R... W9-BIG-372
THE MAGIC OF BELIEVING
HAS DONE FOR OTHERS

"THE MAGIC OF BELIEVING CHANGED MY LIFE. Read it and . . . any problem can be solved, happiness can be achieved, great rewards can be reaped."
—Phyllis Diller

"The reader is almost certain to begin to use latent thought power before he is through many chapters."
—J. A. Zehntbauer,
President,
Jantzen Knitting

"IT OPENS A FIELD OF MENTAL ACTIVITY and accomplishment undreamed of. A very remarkable book."
—Earl Bunting,
past President,
National Association of Manufacturers

"What a help this book should be to young folks in channeling their thoughts to definite goals."
—Homer J. Buckley,
Chairman of the Board,
Homer J. Buckley & Associates

"I personally know of men who have doubled, tripled and quadrupled their income by the use of your theme."
—R. H. Mount,
Business Manager,
Los Angeles Examiner

". . . MUST READING for all who wish to find a way to wider horizons in their business and private lives"
—Ted R. Gamble,
former National Director,
War Finance, U.S. Treasury Department

Most Pocket Books are available at special quantity discounts for bulk purchases for sales promotions, premiums or fund raising. Special books or book excerpts can also be created to fit specific needs.

For details write the office of the Vice President of Special Markets, Pocket Books, 1230 Avenue of the Americas, New York, New York 10020.

THE MAGIC OF BELIEVING

Claude M. Bristol

With an Introduction by Palmer Hoyt,
Editor and Publisher,
The Denver Post, Denver, Colorado;
Member, United States Air Policy Commission.

PUBLISHED BY POCKET BOOKS NEW YORK

POCKET BOOKS, a division of Simon & Schuster, Inc.
1230 Avenue of the Americas, New York, N.Y 10020

Copyright 1948 by Claude M. Bristol

Published by arrangement with Prentice-Hall, Inc.

All rights reserved, including the right to reproduce
this book or portions thereof in any form whatsoever.
For information address Prentice-Hall, Inc.,
Englewood Cliffs, N.J. 07632

ISBN: 0-671-55394-1

First Pocket Books printing October, 1969

20   19   18

POCKET and colophon are registered trademarks
of Simon & Schuster, Inc.

Printed in the U.S.A.

CONTENTS

To
Dr. R. C. W.
who gave me the first clue

To
L. B. N.
who persuaded me to use it

To
E. L. B.
who is a part of it

To
V. P. C. and W. C. B.
*without whose urgings this book
would have never been written*

To
Merton S. Yewdale
*whose friendly advice and enthusiasm
was a constant inspiration*

And To
*the memories of great independent
thinkers of all times this book
is affectionately dedicated.*

"If thou canst believe, all things *are* possible to him that believeth."

Mark 9:23

Introduction

> "The fault, dear Brutus, is
> not in our stars, but in our-
> selves that we are underlings."—
> *Shakespeare*

Generally speaking, people are more interested in themselves and their success than anything else. For this reason
Claude M. Bristol's book, *The Magic of Believing*, ought to
enjoy widest readership.

In simple straightforward language, Mr. Bristol has set
forth some basic principles of the fuller use of the mind in
achieving practical objectives. He has illumined these potential uses with a wealth of descriptive instances, many of them
based on his own personal experiences and observations embracing many years as a newspaper man and a successful
business executive. He has traveled extensively over the world
and has long investigated and studied what he calls "Mind
Stuff."

Claude Bristol has been helping people to help themselves
for twenty years and I have been conversant with what the
author has done with his theme during the period. I am also
conversant with persons mentioned in this interesting book
and with various successes they have achieved.

Mr. Bristol believes deeply that any person can achieve any
given aim if he believes strongly enough, and he presents a
well documented case to prove his point. He makes no claim
to being a "mental healer," but his observations on the relationship of mind to health are of more than passing interest.

The Magic of Believing does not delve into the occult. At
the same time it does not limit the possibilities that telepathy
and the use of the subconscious present.

The Magic of Believing should be an inspiration to anyone
who reads it carefully because, in its development and its

documentation, it is a clear picture of how the great potential possibilities of the mind may be utilized to achieve the ambitions of anyone interested.

Having served in World War I as well as having had a part in the war effort where I came in close contact with service people of World War II, and being aware of potential postwar problems, I should like to see a copy of this book in the hands of every ex-service man and woman as well as all others sincerely interested in making a place for themselves in the years to come.

PALMER HOYT
Editor and Publisher
The Denver Post
Denver, Colorado

THE MAGIC
OF BELIEVING

CHAPTER I

How I Came to Tap the Power of Belief

Is THERE a something, a force, a factor, a power, a science—call it what you will—which a few people understand and use to overcome their difficulties and achieve outstanding success? I firmly believe that there is, and it is my purpose in this, first complete exposition of the subject, to attempt to explain it so that you may use it if you desire.

About fifteen years ago the financial editor of a great Los Angeles newspaper, after attending lectures I had given to financial men in that city and after having read my brochure, *T.N.T.—It Rocks the Earth*, wrote:

"You have caught from the ether something that has a mystical quality—a something that explains the magic of coincidence, the mystery of what makes men lucky."

I realized that I had run across something that was workable, but I didn't consider it then, neither do I now, as anything mystical, except in the sense that it is unknown to the majority of people. It is something that has always been known to a fortunate few down the centuries, but, for some unknown reason, is little understood by the average person.

When I started out years ago to teach this science through the medium of lectures and my brochure, I wasn't certain that it could be or would be grasped by the ordinary individual; but now that I have seen those who have used it double and triple their incomes, build their own successful businesses, acquire homes in the country, and create sizable fortunes, I am convinced that any intelligent person who is sincere with himself can reach any heights he desires. I had no intention of writing a second book, although many urged me to do so, until a woman in the book business, who had sold many copies of my first little book, literally "read the riot act" to me, declaring:

"You have a duty to perform to the ex-service men and women, and all others who seek places for themselves in a postwar world, to give them in easily understood form not only what you contained in your *T.N.T.—It Rocks the Earth* but the new material that you have given in your lectures. Everyone of ambition wants to get ahead and you have amply demonstrated you have something that will help anyone, and it's up to you to pass it along."

It took time to sell myself on the idea, but having served as a soldier in World War I, mostly in France and Germany, and having been an active official for many years in ex-service men's organizations as well as a member of a state commission to aid in the rehabilitation of ex-service men and women, I realized that it would be no easy task for many individuals to make outstanding places for themselves in a practical world from which they had long been separated. It is with them in mind, as well as all ambitious men and women, and with a sincere desire to help, that I write this more full and detailed exposition of the power of belief.

I am cognizant of the fact that there are powerful forces at work in this country that would dominate us, substituting a kind of regimentation for the competitive system which has made America great among nations. They would attempt to destroy individual thinking and initiative, cherished ever since our Pilgrim Fathers established this country in defiance of Old World tyranny. I believe that we must continue to retain the wealth of spirit of our forefathers, for if we don't we shall find ourselves dominated in everything we do by a mighty few and shall become serfs in fact if not in name. Thus this work is written also to help develop individual thinking and doing.

Since I am aware that this book may fall into the hands of some who may call me a "crackpot" or a "screwball," let me say that I am past the half-century mark and have had many years of hard practical business experience, as well as a goodly number of years as a newspaper man. I started as a police reporter, and police reporters are trained to get facts and "accept nothing for granted." For a two-year period I was church editor of a large metropolitan newspaper, during which I came in close contact with clergymen and leaders of all sects and denominations, mind-healers, divine healers, Spiritualists, Christian Scientists, New Thought-ers, Unity leaders, sun and idol worshipers, and, yes, even a few infidels and pagans.

Gypsy Smith, well-known English evangelist, was making an early tour of America at that time, and as I used to sit night after night on his platform, watching people stumble down the aisles, some sobbing, others shouting hysterically, I wondered.

Again I wondered as I accompanied the police in answering a riot call when some Holy Rollers in a moment of hysteria knocked over a stove and set fire to their meeting hall. When I attended my first and only meeting of Shakers, I wondered as I did while attending various spiritualistic meetings. I wondered as I heard the testimonials at the Wednesday night meetings of Christian Scientists. I wondered when I witnessed a group of people being immersed in the icy waters of a mountain stream and coming up shouting "Hallelujah," even though their teeth were chattering. I wondered at the ceremonial dances of the Indians and their rain-calling programs. Billy Sunday also caused me to wonder, as in later years did Aimee Semple McPherson.

In France during the first war I marveled at the simple faith of the peasants and the powers of their village padres. The stories of the so-called miracles at Lourdes, as well as of somewhat similar miracles at other shrines, also held great interest. When I saw elderly men and women in a famous old Roman church climb literally on their knees up a long flight of stairs to gaze upon a holy urn—a climb that is no simple task for an athletically trained young person—I wondered again.

Business brought me into contact with the Mormons, and when I heard of the belief in the story of Joseph Smith and the revelations on the plates of gold, I was again given to wonderment. The Dukhobors of western Canada, who would doff their clothes when provoked, likewise made me wonder. While in Hawaii I heard much about the powers of the kahunas who, it was claimed, could, by praying, cause people to die or live. The great powers attributed to these kahunas profoundly impressed me.

In my early days as a newspaper man I saw a famous medium try to make the "spirits" respond before a crowded courtroom of antagonistic scoffers. The judge had promised the medium he would be freed if he could get the "spirits" to speak in the courtroom. They failed to materialize and I wondered why, because the medium's followers had testified to remarkable prior séances.

Many years later I was commissioned to write a series of articles on what is known in police parlance as the "fortune-telling racket." I visited everything from gypsy phrenologists to crystal-ball gazers, from astrologers to spiritualistic mediums. I have heard what purported to be the voices of old Indian "guides" tell me the past, the present, and the future, and I heard from relatives I never knew existed.

Several times I have been in a hospital room in which people around me died, while others with seemingly worse ailments were up and apparently fully recovered within a short time. I have known of partially paralyzed people who got over their condition in a matter of days. I have known people who claim to have cured their rheumatism or arthritis by wearing a copper band around their wrists—others by mental healing. From relatives and close friends I have heard stories of how warts on hands have suddenly disappeared. I am familiar with the stories of those who permit rattlesnakes to bite them and still live, and with hundreds of other tales of mysterious healings and happenings.

I have, moreover, made myself familiar with the lives of great men and women of history; I have met and interviewed many outstanding men and women in all lines of human endeavor; and I have often wondered just what it was that took them to the top. I have seen coaches take apparently inferior baseball and football teams and infuse them with "something" that caused them to win. In the depression days I saw sales organizations, badly whipped, do an abrupt about-face and bring in more business than ever before.

Apparently I was born with a huge bump of curiosity, for I have always had an insatiable yearning to seek explanations and answers. This yearning has taken me to many strange places, brought to light many peculiar cases, and has caused me to read every book I could get my hands on dealing with religions, cults, and both physical and mental sciences. I have read literally thousands of books on modern psychology, metaphysics, ancient magic, Voodooism, Yogism, Theosophy,

Christian Science, Unity, Truth, New Thought, Couéism, and many others dealing with what I call "Mind Stuff," as well as the philosophies and teachings of the great masters of the past.

Many were nonsensical, others strange, and many very profound. Gradually I discovered that there is a golden thread that runs through all the teachings and makes them work for those who sincerely accept and apply them, and that thread can be named in a single word—*belief*. It is this same element or factor, belief, which causes people to be cured through mental healing, enables others to climb high the ladder of success, and gets phenomenal results for all who accept it. Why belief is a miracle worker is something that cannot be satisfactorily explained; but have no doubt about it, there's genuine magic in believing. "The magic of believing" became a phrase around which my thoughts steadily revolved.

When *T.N.T.—It Rocks the Earth* was first published, I imagined that it would be easily understood, as I had written it simply; but as the years went by I found that some readers protested that it was too much in digest form, while others said they couldn't understand it. I had assumed that most people knew something about the power of thought. I was mistaken, and I realized that those who had an understanding of the subject were comparatively few. Later in my many years of lecturing before clubs, business and sales organizations, I discovered that while most people were vitally interested in the subject, it had to be fully explained. Finally, I undertook to write this book in words that anyone who reads can understand and with the hope that it will help many to reach their goal in life.

The science of thought is as old as man himself. The wise men of all ages have known about it and used it. The only thing the writer has done is to put the subject in modern language and bring to the reader's attention what a few of the outstanding minds of today are doing to substantiate the great truths that have come down through the centuries.

Fortunately for the world, people generally are coming to the realization that there is "something to this mind-stuff after all," and the writer believes that there are millions of people who would like to get a better understanding of it and prove that it does work.

Therefore, I start with relating a few experiences of my own life, with the hope that by hearing them, you will gain a better understanding of the entire science. Early in 1918 I landed in France as a "casual" soldier, unattached to a regular company. As a result it was several weeks before my service record, necessary for my pay, caught up with me. During that period I was without money to buy gum, candy, cigarettes, and the like, as the few dollars I had before sailing had been spent at the transport's canteen to relieve the monotony of the ship's menu. Every time I saw a man light a cigarette or chew a stick of gum, the thought came that I was without money to spend on myself. Certainly, I was eating and the army clothed me and provided me with a place on the ground to sleep, but I grew bitter because I had no spending money and no way of getting any. One night en route to the forward area on a crowded troop train when sleep was out of the question, I made up my mind that when I returned to civilian life, "I would have a lot of money." The whole pattern of my life was altered at that moment.

True, I had been something of a reader in my youth; the Bible had been a "must" in our family. As a boy I was interested in wireless telegraphy, X-ray, high-frequency apparatus, and similar manifestations of electricity, and I had read every book on these subjects I could find. But while I was familiar with such terms as radiations, frequencies, vibrations, oscillations, magnetic influences, etc., in those days they meant nothing to me outside the strictly electrical field. Perhaps the first inkling of a connection between the mind and electrical or vibratory influences came when upon my completing law school an instructor had given me an old book, Thomson Jay Hudson's *Law of Psychic Phenomena*. I read it but only superficially. I either did not understand it or my mind was not ready to receive its profound truths, because, when on that fateful night in the spring of 1918 I told myself that some day I would have a lot of money, I did not realize that I was laying the groundwork for a series of causes which would unleash forces that would bring accomplishment. As a matter of fact, the idea that I could with my thinking and believing develop a fortune never entered my mind.

On my army classification card I was listed as a newspaper man. I had been attending an army training school to qualify for a commission, but the whole training-school course was discontinued just as we finished the course; thus most of us landed in France as enlisted men. However, I considered myself a qualified newspaper man and felt that there was a better place for me in the A.E.F.; yet, like many others, I found myself pushing wheelbarrows and lugging heavy shells and other ammunition. Then one night at an ammunition depot near Toul, things began to happen. I was ordered to appear before the commanding officer who asked me whom I knew at First Army Headquarters. I didn't know a soul there and didn't even know where it was located, and I told him. Then he showed me orders directing me to report immediately to that headquarters. A car and driver were provided and the next morning found me at First Army Headquarters in charge of a daily progress bulletin. There I was answerable only to a colonel.

During the months that followed I frequently thought about the commission to which I was entitled. Then the links began to form into a chain. One day entirely out of a clear sky came orders transferring me to the *Stars and Stripes*, the army newspaper; I had long had an ambition to be on its staff but had done nothing about it. The next day as I was preparing to leave for Paris I was called before the colonel who showed me a telegram signed by the Adjutant General's office at GHQ, asking if I was available for a commission. The colonel asked whether I would rather have a commission than report to the army newspaper. Foreseeing that the war would soon end and I would be happier among other newspaper men, I said I would prefer the transfer to the *Stars and Stripes.* I never learned who was responsible for the telegram, but obviously something was working in my behalf.

Following the armistice, my desire to get out of the army became insistent. I wanted to begin building that fortune, but the *Stars and Stripes* did not suspend publication until the summer of 1919, and it was August before I got home. However, the forces I had unconsciously set in motion were already setting the stage for me and that fortune. It was about nine-thirty the next morning after my arrival home that I received a telephone call from the president of a well-known club in which I had been active. He told me to call a certain man prominent in the investment banking business who had read a newspaper item about my return and had expressed a wish to see me before I resumed newspaper work. I called the man and two days later embarked upon a long career as an investment banker, which later led me to the vice-presidency of a well-known Pacific Coast firm.

While my salary was small at the start, I realized that I was in a business where there were many opportunities to make money. Just how I was to make it was then not revealed, but I "just knew" that I would have that fortune I had in mind. In less than ten years not only did I have it, and it was sizable, but I was a substantial stockholder in the company and had several outside profitable interests. During those years I had constantly before me a mental picture of wealth.

Many people in moments of abstraction or while talking on the telephone engage in what is known as "doodling"—drawing or sketching odd designs and patterns upon paper. My "doodling" was in the form of dollar signs like these "$$$$$—$$$$—$$$—$$" on every paper that came across my desk. The cardboard covers of all the files placed before me daily were scrawled with these markings; so were the covers of telephone directories, scratch-pads, and even the face of important correspondence. I want my readers to have this story, because it suggests the mechanics to be used in applying this magic which will be explained in detail later.

During the past years, I have found that by far the greatest problems bothering most people are financial ones, and in the postwar days with their intense competition, millions are facing the same kind of problems. However, it matters little to what ends this science is used, it will be effective in achieving the object of your desire—and in this connection let me tell another experience.

Shortly after the idea of *T.N.T.—It Rocks the Earth* came to me and before I reduced it to writing, I decided on a trip to the Orient and sailed on the *Empress of Japan,* noted for its excellent cuisine. In my travels through Canada and in Europe I had developed a fondness for "Trappist" cheese (made by the Trappist monks of Quebec), and when I couldn't find it on the ship's menus I complained laughingly to the chief steward that I had sailed on his ship only to get some of the famous "Trappist" cheese. He replied that he was sorry but there was none aboard. The more I thought about it, the more I hungered for some of that cheese. One night a ship's party was held and upon returning to my cabin quarters after midnight I found that a big table had been set up in one of the rooms and on it was the largest cheese I had ever seen. It was "Trappist" cheese. Later I asked the chief steward where he found it and he answered: "I was certain we had none aboard when you first mentioned it, but you seemed so set on having some I made up my mind to search through all the ship's stores. We found it in the emergency storeroom in the bottom of the hold." Something was working for me on that trip, too, for I had no claim to anything but ordinary service. However, I sat at the executive officer's table and was frequently his personal guest in his quarters as well as on inspection trips through the ship.

Naturally the treatment I received made a great impression on me and in Honolulu I often had the thought that it would be nice to receive comparable attention on my journey home on another ship. One afternoon I got the sudden impulse to leave for the mainland; it was about closing time when I appeared at the ticket agency to ascertain what reservations I could get. I was told that a ship was leaving the next day at noon and I could get the only remaining cabin ticket. I purchased it and the next day just a few minutes before noon, as I started up the gangplank, in an offhand manner I said to myself: "They treated you as a king on the *Empress of Japan*. The least you can do here is to sit at the captain's table. Sure, you'll sit at the captain's table."

The ship got under way and as we steamed out of the harbor, word was received from the dining-room steward for passengers to appear in the dining room for assignment to tables. About half the assignments had been made when I came before him. He asked me for my ticket which I placed on the table. He glanced at it and then at me, saying: "Oh yes, table A, seat No. 5." It was the captain's table and I was seated directly across from him. Many things happened aboard that ship which pertain to this subject, the most prominent being a party supposed to be in honor of my birthday—just an idea of the captain's, because my birthday was months off.

Later when I found myself lecturing, I thought it would be well to get a letter from the captain substantiating the story and I wrote him. He replied: "You know sometimes as we go through life, instinctively we get the idea to do this or that. That noon I was sitting in the doorway of my cabin watching the passengers come up the gangplank, and as you came aboard, something told me to seat you at my table. Beyond that I cannot explain, any more than I can explain how I can frequently stop my ship at the right spot at the pier at the first try."

People who have heard the story—people who know nothing about the magic of believing—have declared that it was mere coincidence that the captain selected me. I am certain it wasn't, and I'm also certain that this captain who knows considerable about this science will agree with me. There were dozens of people aboard that ship far more important than I could ever be. I carried nothing to set me apart, being one of those who can pass in a crowd. So obviously it wasn't the clothes I wore or the way I looked that caused the captain to pick me out of several hundred passengers to receive personal attention.

In laying before you this very workable science, I am aware that the subject has been handled before from many angles, largely from religious and metaphysical approaches, but I am also cognizant that many people shy away from anything that smacks of religion, the occult, or the metaphysical. Accordingly, I am presenting it in the language of a business man who believes that sincere thinking, clear writing, and simple language will get any message across to the people.

You have often heard it said that if you believe you can do a thing, you can do it. An old Latin proverb says, "Believe that you have it, and you have it." Belief is the motivating force that enables you to achieve your goal. If you are ill and the thought or belief is imbedded deeply within you that you will recover, the odds that you will do so are all in your favor. It's the belief or the basic confidence within you that brings outward or material results. I speak of normal and mentally composed people. I wouldn't tell a crippled person that he could excel in baseball or football, nor would I tell a woman who was quite plain-looking that she could make herself into a great beauty overnight, since the odds are against it. Yet these things *could* happen, for there have been many remarkable cures; and I firmly believe that when more is learned about the powers of the mind we shall witness many cures deemed impossible today by the medical profession. Finally, I would never discourage anyone; for anything can happen in this life—and that which can help bring it to pass is Hope.

Dr. Alexander Cannon, a distinguished British scientist and physician, whose books on the general subject of thought have stirred up controversy here and abroad, declares that while today a man cannot grow a new leg (as a crab can grow a new claw), he could if the mind of man hadn't rejected the possibility. The eminent scientist claims that if the thought is changed in the innermost depths of the unconscious mind, then man will grow a new leg as easily as the crab grows a new claw. I know that such a statement may sound absurd or at least incredible, but how do we know that it will not be done some day?

Frequently I lunch with a group of medical men, all specialists in various branches of medicine and surgery, and I know that if I voiced such an idea to them it would be suggested that I be examined by a lunacy commission. However, I find that some of these medical men, especially those more recently graduated from our better schools, are no longer closing their ears and minds to the part that thought plays not only in causing functional disturbances in the body, but also in curing them.

A few weeks before this was written, a neighbor came to me to explain how his warts happened to disappear. He said that while a patient at the hospital he had wandered out on the porch where another convalescent patient was conversing with a friend. The friend was saying to the second patient: "So you would like to get rid of the warts on your hand. Well, just let me count them and they'll disappear." My neighbor said he looked at the stranger for a moment, then said: "While you're about it, will you count mine, too?" He did, and my neighbor thought no more about it until he happened to look at his hands one day after he had gone home. "The mess of warts had entirely disappeared!" he told me.

I told this story to a group of doctors one day, and a personal friend, a well-known specialist, grunted, saying: "Preposterous!" However, across the table from him was another doctor who had recently been teaching in a medical school. He came to my aid, declaring that there were many authenticated cases of suggestion having been used to cure warts.

While I was tempted to ask if any of them knew that in January, 1945, the Columbia University's College of Physicians and Surgeons had set up the first psychoanalytic and psychosomatic clinic in this country for the purpose of studying the unconscious mind and the relationship between the mind and the body, I kept silent, for I felt that I was too outnumbered for an argument. I was certain, however, that none of them recalled that several years ago newspapers and medical journals had reported how Heim, a Swiss geologist, had removed warts by suggestion, and had also cited the procedure of Professor Block, another Swiss specialist, in his use of psychology and suggestion for the same purpose.

Since this conversation, considerable publicity has been given to the findings of Dr. Frederick Kalz, noted Canadian authority, who flatly states that suggestion works, in many cases, even to curing warts which are infectious and caused by a virus. In an article appearing in the *Canadian Medical Association Journal* in 1945, Dr. Kalz declared that, "In every country in the world some magic procedures to cure warts are known . . . It may be anything from covering the wart with spider-webs to burying toad eggs on a crossroad at new moon; all these magic procedures are effective, if the patient *believes in them*." In describing the treatment of patients with skin trouble, he says: "I have often prescribed the very same ointment, accompanied by some promising words, which has been tried unsuccessfully by some other medical man, and got credit for a quick cure." He also points out that especially suggestive is X-ray therapy, which works even when the technician fails to switch on the high power. Experiments with systematic fake irradiation bear out this observation. Here in Dr. Kalz's work we see examples of the *magic of believing* actually at work in the curing of warts and the treatment of skin trouble.

Another time my medical friends and I were discussing telepathy and I remarked that some of our greatest students and scholars believed in it, mentioning that the late Dr. Alexis Carrel, member emeritus of the Rockefeller Institute for Medical Research, was not only a thorough believer in the phenomenon but declared that there was definite scientific proof that man could project his thought even at great distances into other minds. This was a few months before the death of the famous scientist.

"Oh, he's just a senile old man," remarked another specialist at the table, a nationally known member of the American Medical Association.

I looked at him with astonishment, for when Dr. Carrel put forth his ideas in that remarkable book, *Man the Unknown*, published in 1935, he was regarded as one of the world's foremost medical scientists and investigators. It will be recalled that he was the holder of the Nobel Prize for his medical research.

I have no quarrel with the medical fraternity. Quite the contrary, for generally its members are sincere, able and open-minded men, and a number, whom I highly esteem, are among my closest friends. However, I have related these stories to emphasize the point that some medical specialists, especially those inclined to restrict their studies to their respective fields, refuse to accept anything that may upset their early teachings and dogmatic beliefs. This resistance is not confined to the medical profession, for there are countless specialists in other lines, including business, who know very little outside of their chosen fields, and whose minds are closed to any idea beyond their limited imagination. Frequently, I have offered to lend books to these various specialists only to be told, upon informing them of the contents, that they were not interested.

This is the paradox. Many apparently well-educated men and women in their respective fields, will, in their broad ignorance, condemn the idea of thought power and will make no endeavor to learn more about it; *and yet every one of them, if successful, has unconsciously made use of it.* Again, many people will believe only what they like to believe or what fits into their own scheme of things, summarily rejecting anything to the contrary. Countless men whose ideas developed the very civilization in which we live today have been hooted at, slandered, and even crucified by the ignoramuses of their times. As I write this book, I think of the words of Marie Corelli, the English novelist, who became world famous in the last century.

"The very idea that any one creature (human) should be

fortunate enough to secure some particular advantage which others, through their own indolence or indifference, have missed is sufficient to excite the envy of the weak or the anger of the ignorant . . . It is impossible that an outsider should enter into a clear understanding of the mystical spiritual-nature world around him and it follows that the teachings and tenets of that spiritual-nature world must be more or less a closed book to such a one—a book, moreover, which he seldom cares or dares to try and open. For this reason the sages concealed much of their profound knowledge from the multitude, because they rightly recognized the limitations of narrow minds and prejudiced opinions . . . What the fool cannot learn he laughs at, thinking that by his laughter he shows superiority instead of latent idiocy."*

However, great investigators and thinkers of the world, including many famous scientists, are in the open today, freely discussing the subject and giving the results of their experiments. The late Charles P. Steinmetz, famous engineer of the General Electric Company, shortly before his death declared: "The most important advance in the next fifty years will be in the realm of the spiritual—dealing with the spirit—thought." Dr. Robert Gault, while professor of Psychology at Northwestern University, was credited with the statement: "We are at the threshold of our knowledge of the latent psychic powers of man."

Much has been written and said about mystical powers, unknown forces, the occult, metaphysics (beyond science), mental physics, psychology (the science of mind), black and white magic, and many kindred subjects, causing most people to believe that they are in the field of the supernatural. Perhaps they are for some, but my conclusion is that the only inexplicable thing about these powers is that it is belief that makes them work.

During the years that I have appeared before luncheon clubs, business concerns, and sales organizations, as well as talking over the radio to thousands of people about this science, I have seen results that can be termed phenomenal. And, as said previously, many who have used it in their

---

*From *The Life Everlasting* by Marie Corelli, Borden Publishing Co., Los Angeles.

business have doubled, trebled, and quadrupled their incomes. In some cases, even greater returns have been noted. My files are filled with letters from people in all walks of life, testifying what they have accomplished by using the science. As an instance, I think of Ashley C. Dixon, whose name is known to thousands of radio listeners in the Pacific Northwest and who a number of years ago wrote me voluntarily that it had enabled him to make more than $100,000. He said that he had studied this subject in an academic way, but had never fully believed it until he was forty-three, when with only $65 to his name, without employment, and no jobs available, he set out to prove to himself that the science would work. Mr. Dixon has given me permission to use his letter, from which I quote the following excerpts:

"Along came your book *T.N.T.* It put forth in workable form all that I had known before. It was like seeing Niagara Falls for the first time. One knew there was such a place; but confirmation was the actual personal contact with it. And so, *T.N.T.* gave me in print the facts I had known and used, but in a clear form. Here was something I could read and use day by day. Holding the thoughts till they were fully demonstrated.

"What has all this been worth to me in dollars and cents? That, of course, is the question of the average man. He wants to see something which will show up in the profit column; something material in the way of dollars and cents. Here's the answer. Since I was forty-three, broke and needing food for the family, I have made a hundred thousand dollars. Most of it is in paid-up insurance and annuities. I have sold my business which cost me $5000 (originally borrowed) for $30,000 and am now working on a contract to run for the next ten years which will net me $50,000, if I loaf; and more if I care to work. This is not a boast. It is a factual statement of what has actually happened in the past ten years . . . It cannot be done in a moment, or a day or a month, but it can be done."

In 1934, during the lowest point of the so-called depression, the head of the Better Business Bureau in one of the large Pacific Coast cities heard of what was happening to firms and individuals who were following my teachings. He decided to investigate my work. Later he congratulated me publicly and subsequently wrote me as follows:

"My statement that the teachings have done more to stimulate business here during the past year than any other single factor or agency is based upon statements to me by numerous executives who have been using the theme successfully in their business . . . When I first heard of the phenomenal results you were obtaining I was inclined to question the facts—they seemed too preposterous to be true—but upon investigation, talking with heads of firms using the theme and with salesmen who have doubled and trebled their incomes, as well as hearing many of your lectures and getting into the subject myself, the terrific and dynamic force embraced by it all becomes apparent. It isn't going to be understood by everyone in a minute, but the firms and individuals that will accept what you have to give and will follow through can expect some startling and extraordinary results. You have fully demonstrated that, and therefore are to be congratulated for giving others what you caught."

This man has since risen to great heights in the business world in another city and has recently written me of having seen other practical demonstrations of the workings of this science.

As I started this book, I decided to check with some of the individuals and firms who had previously written me certifying to the phenomenal results which they had achieved by using this science. Without exception every one testified to the continuing progress he had made from the time he had first written to me. One of the most outstanding accounts is related by Mr. Dorr Quayle, whose name is well-known to the Disabled American War Veterans, and who has long been active in veterans' affairs in the Northwest. In 1937, he wrote me:

"It was no easy matter, at first, to completely accept your ideas, but my circumstances and physical condition forced me to keep at it continuously until understanding came. This, in itself, was a demonstration. You see, in February, 1924, I was stricken with partial paralysis of my lower limbs which made it necessary to use crutches to even get about at all, and at best, for only very short distances and at a snail's pace. For one who had been active in the business world [a bank executive] this forced inactivity was not easy to get used to. But it was bearable only because I received compensation from our Government—my disability being considered as due to service during the World War. However, in 1933, the Government changed its mind and dropped me from the compensation rolls and I was forced to make a living. My home and other properties were about to go from my possession. It was not a pleasant picture nor a hopeful future.

"Necessity forced me to put into practice the principles so well explained by you. Sticking to it proves them. Possibly I was favored because I could not quit the insurance and public accounting business I had started due to my inability to enter any other kind of work on account of my disability. But persistence gives confidence and continued right mental attitude followed by consistent action will bring success. I have not reached the degree of success I desire, but that does not bother me at all for now I am making a good living, have saved my properties, and know the formula that leads to the fullest success. When you have that knowing *inside* of you, fear has vanished and the obstruction to a continued life of all good, removed."

When I first met Mr. Quayle, it was just after he had started his business with one desk in the front of a plumbing shop. In the following years it has been a pleasure to see him move from place to place, his business growing by leaps and bounds, until today he occupies the entire ground floor of a building on one of the main thoroughfares of a great western city. Realizing that his story of achievement was a remarkable one, I asked for permission to quote his earlier letter. He replied:

"By all means, do so, if you think it will help others. By the way you might add, that I now have the whole quarters at Twentieth and Sandy and I employ twenty-two people. I have just bought the business lot between Twenty-eighth and Twenty-ninth on Sandy where I shall build my own office building. It is my sincere wish that all people would accept your teachings."

I had no idea at the time I grasped this science that I was later to put it into book form. My primary thought was to use it to save my own organization from bankruptcy; I was then vice-president of a well-known investment banking firm. We had been caught in the economic crisis and were headed for disaster. I don't know whether I was inspired or not, but I do know that I dictated the first draft of my brochure in its entirety in less than five hours, without notes or references of any kind before me. At the same time the idea for the brochure came to me, the words, "cosmic consciousness," floated before my mind; but they meant nothing then. It was only after *T.N.T.—It Rocks the Earth* had been published and had reached the hands of a woman author living in New York that I understood the significance of the words, "cosmic consciousness." She wrote me as follows:

"Seriously, it happens that I've been eating and sleeping that philosophy [the one outlined in *T.N.T.*] for the last ten years. It brought me to New York on no carfare; it sold my stuff to publishers when I had a lousy little job earning $30 a week . . . It took me to Europe a couple of times, and bought me silver foxes."

In the same letter she urged me to read Dr. Richard Maurice Bucke's *Cosmic Consciousness,* declaring that it contained brilliant accounts of the actual experience of illumination. I did and I was astounded to discover that my experience actually paralleled the illuminations listed and explained by Dr. Bucke. In the original draft of my brochure I had described in detail my experience with "brilliant white light," but subsequently toned it down, for when I showed the manuscript to a close friend, he urged me to change the wording, declaring: "People will not know what you are talking about in referring to that 'white light'—some may think you've gone off the deep end." Consequently, I changed it; but those of you who know something about "cosmic illumination" and have read my earlier small book will catch my reference to the "light," even though I did somewhat obscure the picture in accordance with the suggestion of my friend. However, the memory of that signal experience will always remain, for in those few seconds I received more knowledge and understanding than I had ever received in my years of reading and studying.

It was in the same period that it came to me in a flash that the reason my firm was going on the rocks was not because of the threatening outside happenings and events, but because of the mental attitude of its members and employees. We were all succumbing to mass fear thoughts; we feared that the depression was weakening our spirit and sweeping everything downhill to financial disaster, and with our own thoughts of ruin we were attracting the disaster to ourselves. It occurred to me that all I needed to do to save the firm and to begin fighting the depression itself was to reverse the thinking of every person connected with our organization. I set about doing that very thing; and, as Frank W. Camp who wrote the introduction to my brochure declared, it was followed "by the most remarkable transformation of individuals and organization as well."

I am aware that some of my statements may be ridiculed by classroom psychologists, but nevertheless in America today there are thousands of people daily demonstrating for themselves that the science works. As for you, the reader, the main point to consider is whether or not it will work for you, and the only way you can demonstrate it is to *try it yourself.*

In using this science, which is given you with confident knowledge that no matter how you use it you will get results, I wish to repeat a warning given in my brochure: *Never use it for harmful or evil purposes.*

Since the beginning of man there have been two great subtle forces in the world—good and evil. Both are terrifically powerful in their respective scopes and cycles. The basic principle operating both is *mind power*—massed mind power. Sometimes evil appears to have the upper hand, and at other times good is at the controls. It is mind power that has built empires, and now we have seen how it can be used to destroy them—history is recording the facts.

If you read this book reflectively, you will understand how the science can be used with terribly destructive force, as well as for good and constructive results. It is like many natural forces, e.g., water and fire, which are among men's greatest benefactors. Yet both can be hideously catastrophic, depending upon whether they are used for constructive or destructive purposes.

Therefore, take great care that you do not misuse the science of "Mind Stuff." I cannot emphasize this too strongly, for if you employ it for harmful or evil purposes, it will

boomerang and destroy you just as it has others down through
the centuries. These are not idle words, but solemn words of
warning.

CHAPTER II

Mind-Stuff Experiements

IN ORDER to get a clearer understanding of our subject, the
reader should give thought to thought itself and to its phenomena. No one knows what thought really is, other than it is
some sort of mental action; but, like the unknown element,
electricity, we see its manifestations everywhere. We see it in
the actions and expressions of a child, in an aged person, in
animals, and, in fact, to varying degrees in every living thing.
The more we contemplate and study thought, the more we
realize what a terrific force it is and how unlimited are its
powers.

Glance around as you read this. If you are in a furnished
room, your eyes tell you that you are looking at a number of
inanimate objects. That is true so far as visual perception is
concerned; but in reality you are actually looking at thoughts
or ideas which have come into materialization through the
creative work of some human being. It was a thought, first,
that created the furniture, fashioned the window glass, gave
form to the draperies and coverings.

The automobile, the skyscraper, the great planes that sweep
the stratosphere, the sewing machine, the tiny pin, a thousand
and one things—yes, millions of objects—where did they
come from originally? Only one source. From that strange
force—thought. As we analyze further, we realize that these
achievements, and in fact all of our possessions, came as a
result of creative thinking. Ralph Waldo Emerson declared
that the ancestor of every action is thought; when we understand that, we begin to comprehend that our world is gov-
erned by thought and that everything without had its counter-

part originally within the mind. It is just as Buddha said many centuries ago: "All that we are is the result of what we have thought."

Your very life is your thinking and the result of your thinking processes. Your flesh, bones, and muscles can be reduced to 70 per cent water and a few chemicals of small value, but it is your mind and what you think that makes you what you are. The secret of success lies not without, but within, the thoughts of man.

Figuratively, thought makes giants out of pigmies, and often turns giants into pigmies. History is filled with accounts of how thought has made weak men strong and strong men weak, and we see evidence of its working around us constantly.

You do not eat, wear clothes, run for a bus, drive your automobile, go for a walk, or read a newspaper—you don't even raise your arm—without a preceding thought impulse. While you may consider the motions you make as more or less automatic, perhaps caused by some physical reflexes, behind every single step you take in life, regardless of its direction, is that formidable and powerful force—thought.

The very way you walk, the way you carry yourself, your talk, your manner of dress, all reflect your way of thinking. A slovenly carriage is an indication of slovenly thinking, whereas an alert, upright carriage is the outward sign of inward strength and confidence. What you exhibit outwardly, you are inwardly. You are the product of your own thought. What you believe yourself to be, you are.

Thought is the original source of all wealth, all success, all material gain, all great discoveries and inventions, and of all achievement. Without it there would be no great empires, no great fortunes, no great transcontinental rail lines, no modern conveniences; in fact, there would be no advance over life in the most primitive ages.

Your thoughts, those that predominate, determine your character, your career, indeed your everyday life. Thus it becomes easy to understand what is meant by the statement that a man's thoughts make or break him. And when we realize that there can be no action or reaction, either good or bad, without the generating force of thought initiating it, the Biblical saying, "For whatsoever a man soweth, that shall he also reap," and Shakespeare's words, "There is nothing either good or bad, but thinking makes it so," become more intelligible.

Sir Arthur Eddington, the famous English physicist, says that to an altogether unsuspected extent the universe in which we live is a creation of our minds; while the late Sir James Jeans, who was equally famous in the same field, suggested that the universe was merely a creation that resulted from the thought of some great universal mind underlying and coordinating all of our minds. Nothing is clearer than that the world's greatest scientists and thinkers of our age are not only voicing the ideas of the wisest men of old, but that they are confirming the fundamental principle of this book.

Almost since the beginning of the human race, the molding of men has been done by those who knew something of thought's great power. All the great religious leaders, kings, warriors, statesmen have understood this science and have known that people act as they think and also react to the thought of others, especially when it is stronger and more convincing than their own. Accordingly, men of powerful dynamic thought have ever swayed the people by appealing to their minds, sometimes to lead them into freedom and sometimes into slavery. There never was a period in history when we should study our own thoughts more, try to understand them, and learn how to use them to improve our position in life, by drawing upon the great source of power that lies within each of us.

There was a time when I would have laughed at people who talked about the magnetic force of thought, how thought correlates with its object, how it can affect people and inanimate things, even at great distances. But I no longer laugh, nor do others who know something of its power, for anyone who has any intelligence sooner or later comes to the realization that thought can change the surface of the entire globe.

The late George Russell, famous Irish editor and poet, was quoted as saying that we become what we contemplate. Undoubtedly, we become what we envisage, and he certainly demonstrated it in his own life by becoming a great writer, lecturer, painter, and poet.

However, it must be borne in mind that many of our ideas, the thoughts we think, are not ours at all, or those of our own originating. We are molded also by the thoughts of others; by what we hear in our social life, what we read in newspapers, magazines, and books, what we hear in the movies, the theater, and on the radio; even by chance remarks from the conversation of bystanders—and these thoughts bombard us constantly. Some of them that accord with our own inmost thoughts and also open the way to greater visions in our life are helpful. But often there are thoughts that are upsetting, that weaken our self-confidence, and turn us away from our high purposes. It is these outside thoughts that are the trouble makers, and later I shall point out how you can keep free of them.

Few people give much thought to the law of cause and effect as applicable to the operation of the mind, or comprehend what is meant when they hear such thoughts as, "Everything is within; nothing is without" or "Mind is the source of all power," and so on. I believe that no better explanation of this can be given than appeared in an article published in the *Commercial and Financial Chronicle* (Dec. 10, 1932). This publication has been known for more than a hundred years as the "Bible of business and finance," and with the permission of Herbert D. Seibert, editor and publisher, I quote it in part. It is entitled "El Dorado."

El Dorado, a country rich beyond all precedent in gold and jewels, lies at every man's door. Your bonanza lies under your feet. Your luck is ready at hand. All is within; nothing is without, though it often appears that men and peoples by dumb luck or avarice or force or over-reaching strike upon the sea of prosperity . . . Man individually and collectively is entitled to life in all abundance. It is a most evident fact. Religion and philosophy assert it; history and science prove it. "That they might have life, and that they might have it more abundantly," is the law. What do you seek? Pay the price and take it away. There is no limit to the supply, but the more precious the thing you seek the higher the price. For everything we obtain we must barter the gold of our own spirits . . .

Where to find the gold of the All Powerful? One secures the gold of the spirit when he finds himself. When he finds himself, he finds freedom and all riches, achievement, and prosperity. High sounding talk? No, the most palpable evidence of American history and biography, of all history. The concrete proof is apparent even in current events if we but open our eyes. Nothing substantial, lasting, powerful, or moving was ever accomplished, nor ever can be, except which commands dominion, power, and accomplishment. Men who know themselves know at once that all material things and ideas have a spiritual counterpart or basis. They see it in money, in credit. The law of supply and demand is not to an awakened man merely an economic principle, but the material manifestation of spiritual law. Such freedom-seeking men see the same principle operating in gravitation, in chemical affinities, in macrocosm and in microcosm . . .

America has long been the greatest of El Dorados, the stage upon which the most numerous of self-found men worked their bonanzas and their miracles of thought to the enrichment of themselves and mankind at large. There is no exploitation, only a showering of gifts, easily bought by free spirits and generously scattered on all hands according to the expressed law of bargain of the Original, Permanent Owner, and First Producer. To the self-found man of action all the money, credit, and capital goods he can use . . . Mackay, O'Brien, Hearst, and Fair, brave young Americans of 1849, found gold in themselves before they struck it rich in California. They had to. "If there is gold there," they told one another, "we'll get our share" . . . How great must have been the spiritual wealth of such a free-found man as James J. Hill, who built the Great Northern Railroad from nowhere to nowhere, in a wilderness where no one lives. His madness founded an empire. By spiritual force he turned forests and plains into a thousand El Dorados, and by the same force commanded all the gold and credit needed for the markets of Amsterdam and London and enabled millions of Americans to discover for themselves great bonanzas in the cold Northwest.

Thomas A. Edison said a few years before he died: "Ideas come from space. This may seem astonishing and impossible to believe, but it is true. Ideas come from out of space." Surely Edison should have known, for few men ever received or gave forth more ideas . . . Let each man seek the El Dorado within himself. Power is plentiful. The source is inexhaustible. As the Canonical Fathers of the church expressed it, that which is received is according to the measure of the recipient. It is not the power that is lacking, it is the will. When one finds oneself the will becomes automatically set toward El Dorado.

By a full and powerful imagination anything can be brought into concrete form. The great physician, Paracelsus, said: "The human spirit is so great a thing that no man can express it; could we rightly comprehend the mind of man nothing would be impossible to us upon the earth. Through faith the imagination is invigorated and completed, for it really happens that every doubt mars its perfection. Faith must strengthen the imagination, for faith establishes the will." Faith is personal, individual. Salvation, any way you take it, is personal. Faith comes in the finding of one's self. This self-finding establishes a clear realization of one's identity with the eternal. Strong, self-assertive men built up this El Dorado of America. "Man, know thyself," thine own individual self, is everlastingly the supreme command. Self-knowers always dwell in El Dorado; they drink from the fountain of youth, and are at all times owners of all they wish to enjoy.

The words of Paracelsus just quoted are well worth rereading and further study, for once you grasp their meaning and discover how to apply the principle, you will certainly have more light on how to succeed in your undertakings. However, I would like to point out that hard work alone will not bring success. The world is filled with people who have worked hard but have little to show for it. Something more than hard work is necessary: it is creative thinking and firm belief in your ability to execute your ideas. The successful people in history have succeeded through their thinking. Their hands were merely helpers to their brains.

Another important point is that one essential to success is that your desire be an all-obsessing one, your thoughts and aims be co-ordinated, and your energy be concentrated and applied without letup. It may be riches or fame or position or knowledge that you want, for each person has his own idea of what success means to him. But whatever you consider it to be, you can have it provided you are willing to make the objective the burning desire of your life. A big order, you say. Not at all; by using the dynamic force of believing, you can set all your inner forces in motion, and they in turn will help you to reach your goal. If you are married, you remember the stimulating and emotional experience of courting the girl you wanted for your wife. Certainly, it wasn't nerve-racking work —quite the contrary, you'll admit—but what were you using, if not this very same science, even though unconsciously. The desire to win a helpmate was uppermost in your mind from the time you got the idea until your marriage. The thought, the belief, was with you every minute of the day and perhaps it was with you in your dreams.

Now that you have a clearer idea of the part that thought and desire play in our daily lives, the first thing to determine is precisely what you want. Starting in with the general idea that you merely want to be a success, as most people do, is too indefinite. You must have a mental pattern clearly drawn in your mind. Ask yourself, Where am I headed? What is my goal? Have I visualized just what I really want? If success is to be measured in terms of wealth, can you fix the amount in figures? If in terms of achievement, can you specify it definitely?

I ask these questions, for in their answers are factors which will determine your whole life from now on. Strange as it may appear, not one out of a hundred people can answer these questions. Most people have a general idea that they would like to be a success, but beyond that everything is vague. They merely go along from day to day figuring that if they have a job today they will have it tomorrow, and that somehow they will be looked after in their old age. They are like a cork on the water floating aimlessly, drawn this way and that by various currents, and either being washed up on the shore, or becoming waterlogged and eventually sinking.

Therefore, it is vital that you know exactly what you want out of life. You must know where you are headed, and you must keep a fixed goal in view. That, of course, is the over-all picture; it makes no difference whether you want *a* job or a *better* one, a new house, a place in the country, or just a new pair of shoes. You must have a fixed idea before you'll obtain what you are after.

There is a great difference between a need and a desire. For example, you may *need* a new car for business, and you may *desire* one in order to give pleasure to your family. The one for your business you will get as a matter of necessity. The one for your family you will plan to get as soon as possible. For this car you will make an extra effort, because it is something you have never had before, something that will add to your responsibilities, and something that will compel you to seek new powers within yourself and new resources outside. It is desire for something new, something different, something that is going to change your life, that causes you to make an extra effort; and it is the *power of believing* that alone sets in motion those inner forces by which you add what I call *plus-values* to your life.

So you begin with desire if you ever hope to achieve anything or gain more than you have now. It is the prime motivating force in all of us and, without an all-consuming desire, nothing can be achieved or gained. However, as we shall see, there is more to it than mere desire.

I am aware that metaphysicians claim that thoughts are things. They may be in a general sense; but, so far as the effect upon us individually is concerned, they do not become real to us until we give them life with our own thinking or through the workings of our imaginations.

At first reading, this may appear a little strange but it will perhaps become clearer if I cite a few examples. For instance, you are advised to wear rubbers when you go out in the rain. We've all heard the remark, "If you don't, you'll catch your death of cold." That thought has never had the slightest effect upon me. I haven't worn rubbers since I was a small child. I have had my shoes and feet thoroughly wet hundreds of times and often for hours at a time, yet I cannot recall the time I ever caught cold as a result. Some people have a tremendous fear of drafts, but I have often thought that if they did catch cold by being in a draft it was because of the fear thoughts rather than because of the drafts themselves. I sit in drafts for long periods daily, and at night I sleep in a corner room which has windows on both sides of the room that I raise in all sorts of weather, so that the wind often sweeps across me. Yet I've never had a cold as a result, because I never give it a thought.

However, I do not advise anyone accustomed to wearing rubbers to go without them, neither do I suggest to anyone afraid of drafts to stay in them. For lifelong habits and beliefs with their consequences are not going to change overnight.

For centuries outstanding thinkers have claimed that man through his mind could shape events and control matter, and the more you study this science, the more you will realize the amazing powers of your own mind.

A. Conan Doyle, creator of Sherlock Holmes, and for many years a member of the British Society for Psychic Research, declared that he believed there was a constructive and destructive power in thought alone which was akin to the "faith that can move mountains." He said that while the results themselves were conclusive, he had no idea what power it was that came from a man's mind and that could separate the molecules of a solid object toward which it was directed. I know that materialists will scoff at such a statement. But just remember what is being done with radar and how radio waves go through wood, brick, steel, and other so-called solid objects. If thought waves, or whatever they are, can be tuned to even higher oscillations, why can't they affect the molecules of solid objects?

There are many professional gamblers who contend that a strong mental influence has much to do with achieving so-called lucky results in games of chance, such as card playing, the calling of dice, the operation of a roulette wheel, etc. The writer knows one man who can step up to a cigar store punchboard and with a few punches grab off the best prizes. Once I asked him about it and he said: "I never go near a punchboard unless I am in the mood for it, and that means that I must be in the frame of mind that I'm going to win. I've noticed that if there's the slightest doubt in my mind, I don't win. But I can't recall the time that I didn't get winning numbers when the winning idea was firmly fixed in my mind before I started to play."

Hooey, you say—but wait. Do you know that departments of psychology in great universities have already undertaken experiments to determine whether the mind possesses the power to influence material objects, and that the experiments have already demonstrated the existence of such a power? While the experiments have not been too widely publicized, there have been stories appearing from time to time giving the general facts.

Perhaps the most outstanding work has been done at Duke University, where Dr. J. B. Rhine and his associates have demonstrated that psychokinesis, the name given to designate the power of mind by which material objects are influenced, is much more than idle theory. Dice (yes, the old army type of dice used in crap games) were thrown by a mechanical device to eliminate all possibility of personal influence and trickery. Since 1934 when experiments of this type were started, there have been many tests in which millions of throws of the dice have been made. The results were such as to cause Dr. Rhine to declare that "there is no better explanation than the subjects influenced the fall of the dice without any recognized physical contacts with them." By mentally concentrating upon the appearance of certain numbers, while at the same time they stood at a distance to avoid all physical contact with the mechanical thrower and with the dice, the experimenters were frequently able to control the dice. In a number of the experiments, the scores made under psychokinesis refuted some of the traditional mathematical odds of millions to one against the reappearance of certain combinations of numbers in repeated succession.

Meditate over this for a few minutes and then realize what it means to you. Those experiments give you some idea of what is meant by "Thought creates after its kind," "Thought correlates with its object," "Thought attracts that upon which it is directed," and similar statements that we have heard for years. Recall that it was Job who said: "For the thing which I greatly feared is come upon me." Our fear thoughts are just as creative or just as magnetic in attracting troubles to us as are the constructive and positive thoughts in attracting positive results. So no matter what the character of the thought, it does create after its kind. When this sinks into a man's consciousness, he gets some inkling of the awe-inspiring power which is his to use.

However, I cling to the theory that while thoughts do create and exercise control far beyond any limits yet known to man, they create only according to their pitch, intensity, emotional quality, depth of feeling, or vibratory plane. In other words, comparable to the wave length and wattage of a radio station, thoughts have a creative or controlling force in the exact ratio of their constancy, intensity, and power.

While many explanations have been offered, no one knows whether thought is a form of electrical energy or something else yet to be defined. But having been an experimenter in that branch of electricity known as "high-frequency," in which the great electrical genius, Nicola Tesla, pioneered, whenever I think of thought and its radiations or vibrations, I instinctively link them up with electricity and its phenomena. In this manner they become more understandable to me.

I find that I am far from being alone in holding this idea, for scientists have perfected apparatus that actually charts the oscillations of the vibration emanating from the human brain. The apparatus up to this time has been used primarily to indicate a person's mental health, but investigators declare that shadings of emotions, dreams, and remote disease are also considered and studied.

In 1944, Dr. H. S. Burr and his co-workers at Yale University, after experimenting for twelve years, reached the conclusion that an electrical aura of their own making surrounds all living things, and that life is connected electrically to the whole pattern of the universe. For years, mystics, occultists, and metaphysicians have claimed that each individual possesses such an aura, and there are countless cases in which these auras have been recorded as actually seen. However, in no instance, until the results at Yale were published, have I found an explanation in which these are linked with electrical phenomena.

Hermes Trismegistus and the ancient Hermetic philosophers all taught the theory of vibration, while Pythagoras, the great geometrician and philosopher, who lived in the sixth century before Christ, held that everything that exists is a vibration This is the very essence of our scientific electronic theory of today—that all matter consists of electrons (negative) and protons (positive), that is, of particles or charges of electricity which are constantly acting and reacting upon each other. For lack of a better term, I use the word "vibration" or "oscillation," and when the "frequency" of the electrical particles is changed, the form of material object changes. The difference in matter and the so-called solids as we know them is the difference in the composition of the vibrations—the electrons and the protons. Herein we have a possible explanation of the forces used by the ancient alchemists who claimed to be able to transmute the lesser elements and metals into those of greater value: e.g., iron and lead into silver and gold. They claimed also to be able to heal all disease by the same forces. Rutherford, an English physicist, well known for his research into radioactivity, has thrown some light on this theory of transmutation of the elements and the lesser metals in connection with the theory of electronics.

When we realize that our nervous system is reached only through vibration, in other words, that our five known and defined senses record seeing, hearing, feeling, tasting, and smelling by means of the vibrations given off by the external things themselves, we get a better understanding of the nature of vibrations. For example, we hear a loud noise. It comes to us only via the sound vibration. We see a green leaf, but it is merely the color vibration as gathered by the eyes, and later transmitted to the brain. There are, however, many vibrations which are pitched at a much greater frequency than our five senses are attuned to, and of which we never have any conscious knowledge. By way of illustration, there is a dog whistle pitched so high that only a dog can hear it.

We have all heard of the power of "the laying on of hands," and most of us know how soothing hands stroking our temples can lessen the intensity of a headache. Can this be due to some form of electrical energy flowing from our finger ends? The Bible tells of numerous instances where healing was accomplished by the touch of Jesus' hand. Does the explanation lie in this little-known field of electricity—the science of vibration? And does this electrical atmosphere, which Dr. Burr claims is of our own making and which surrounds all living things, enable us to cause certain impulses to pour forth literally from our fingers or from our minds—vibratory forces that can act upon others and upon so-called material objects? All persons living in high altitudes have felt and sometimes observed the electric spark resulting from walking across the room and then touching some metallic substance. That, of course, is a form of static electricity generated by friction, but it gives an idea of how one kind of electricity can be developed through the body.

Among pictures descriptive of the experiments of Yale investigators is one showing that when intact forefingers (that is, without cuts or other injuries) were dipped in salt-water cups connected with a galvanometer, there was a flow of electricity between the positive left hand and the negative right hand, measuring 1.5 millivolts. In another picture, two middle fingers, one with a slight cut at the tip, were partially immersed in the cups, but this time the polarity of the hands changed, the left hand changing from positive to negative and the right becoming positive, with the current stepping up to 12 millivolts.

As I looked at those pictures, I recalled an instrument known as a "biometre" perfected many years ago by a French scientist, Dr. Hippolyte Baraduc, consisting of a bell-shaped glass in which was suspended a copper needle fastened to a fine silk thread. Below the needle but inside the glass was a circular piece of cardboard marked off into degrees.

Two of these instruments were placed side by side and the fingers of both hands of the operator were held within half an inch of the glasses, his mind concentrated on the delicately balanced needle. By changing his mental attitude or the polarity of his thinking, the operator could cause corresponding changes in the direction of the needle, now in one direction and now in another, the needle following absolutely his changing directive thought currents.

Here is a simple experiment embodying similar principles. Take a piece of medium-weight paper, about three inches square, and fold it diagonally from corner to corner. Then open it and make another diagonal fold so that there will be two folds or creases forming intersecting diagonals. Again open the paper, which will now present the appearance of a low, partially flattened-out pyramid. Now take a long needle and force it through a cork so that the point extends an inch or so above the top side of the cork. Place the cork with its needle, point up, on top of an inverted water glass, so that there may be free movement of both hands and of the paper which is to revolve on the needle point. Then take the piece of paper and balance it, where the creases intersect, on the point of the needle, placing it so that the four sides of the pyramid point downward.

Place the glass, with the cork, needle, and paper on a table or desk in a room free from drafts, keeping away from heat registers or windows, thus avoiding possible heat waves or air currents. Then place the hands around the piece of paper in a semi-cupped position, keeping the hands or fingers a half inch or so away from the paper, so that it may revolve freely. Now order it to revolve upon the needle point. At first it will wobble—perhaps revolving slowly at first and in one direction or the other; but if your hands remain steady and you concentrate upon a certain direction of movement, the paper will revolve until it turns rapidly upon the needle point. If you mentally order a change in direction, the one-way movement will cease and the paper will start revolving in the opposite direction. Of course, it is essential that you do not breathe or exhale in the direction of the paper.

Many explanations of what causes the paper to revolve have been offered, such as heat waves from the hands, a body reflex of some kind, and the like. If the paper revolved in only one direction, then one of these explanations could be accepted. But when a person, with a little practice and confident and concentrated thinking, can cause the paper to revolve first in one direction and then in another by reversing the polarity of his thinking, it is clear that the principle is the same as that which governs the experiments with the biometre.

In carrying out another similar experiment, a small disc of cardboard known as the "dialette" bearing the facsimile of the face of a clock, with numbers from one to twelve, is used. (This is better known as the Rosicrucian Dialette and is issued by Amorc, Rosicrucian Brotherhood.) A sharp needle is pushed through its center and on top of it is balanced a sliver of thin cardboard fashioned in the shape of an arrow. The disc is placed on top of a glass filled with water in which the lower part of the needle is submerged. The operator places his hands around the top of the glass, the disc, and arrow; then orders the arrow to revolve, change its position, or stop at any desired position or number. However, it must be recognized in all these experiments that not everyone can immediately get satisfactory results, because the power of mind or thought concentration and projective influence varies in individuals.

If there is a form of electricity which emanates from our hands or fingers in particular and if there are waves, either dynamic or magnetic, caused by vibrations set up either consciously or unconsciously by our thinking, do we not then have an explanation of table-lifting, automatic writing, the performances of the planchette or ouija board, and many of the mediumistic or occult operations? Now that the Yale experimenters have concluded that all living things are surrounded by an electrical atmosphere of their own making, and the Duke experimenters are still exploring the field for further proof that thought or some similar force can affect material objects, we are beginning to receive verification of the idea expressed by Dr. Phillips Thomas, research engineer for the Westinghouse Electric Company. In 1937, according to newspaper dispatches, Dr. Thomas told the Utah session of the American Electrical Institute:

"We feel certain that whatever we do, say, or think is accomplished by some type of radiation. We think such radiations are electricity. In the near future we may be able to capture and interpret these radiations of personality and thought through electrical impulses. Prospects of an early solution are bright."

Since some of my readers may not have a clear understanding of the radiation of thought, I offer a simple explanation. A pebble tossed into a pond immediately upon striking the surface of the water sets up a series of ripples or small waves, which spread out circle-like and ultimately reach the shore line where they appear to stop. The larger the pebble, the higher the waves. Two stones of different sizes and weights tossed in simultaneously at different places but in close proximity will both set up a series of waves, converging upon each other. Where the two sets meet there appears to be a struggle as to which is to overcome or pass the other. As far as our physical vision is concerned, if the waves are of the same size, both seem to stop or merge at their meeting-point; but if one is larger than the other, the larger sweeps over the smaller and creates waves in the wake of the smaller ripples.

Think about this in connection with your own mental impulses—for example, how thoughts of one nature stop or overwhelm others—and you readily appreciate how the more powerful or concentrated the thought, the quicker its tempo, the greater its vibration, the more it sweeps aside the weaker vibrations, the more rapidly it does its creative work.

We hear and read much about various stages of thought, degrees of consciousness, thought concentration, the strength of our faith, all of which deals with the intensity or the degree of power we send forth. Creative force comes only when there is a completely rounded-out thought, when there is a fully developed mental picture, or when the imagination can visualize the fulfillment of our ambition and see in our mind a picture of the object we desire—a house, a car, a radio, etc.—just as if we already possessed them.

As a result of my studies of the so-called mystic teachings, the various mental sciences and the regular orthodox church teachings, I am convinced that they all work in varying degrees, but only to the extent that their followers believe. So it is with prayer, whether it be a part of a church service or the purely spontaneous and personal supplication of the individual.

However, I am forced to the conclusion that many people go through the lip-service act of saying their prayers without the slightest belief that those prayers will be answered. Consequently, they are not answered. I am frequently reminded of the story of the old lady who, professing a belief in prayer, undertook to go shopping. The day before she prayed that on her shopping day the sun would shine. But upon completion of her prayer she glanced out of the window, saw some black clouds, and instantly declared: "But I know it's going to rain."

In the late fall of 1944, the *Saturday Review of Literature,* which doesn't go in for hocus-pocus, contained an article by Thomas Sugrue. He declared that the mind-cure movement had grown so rapidly that it was now encountered everywhere. He cited several cases in which both men and women had secured phenomenal results. One woman, who at sixty-two had been partially crippled and whose fingers were bent with arthritis, had taken up a system of Yogi breathing and had entirely recovered from her physical ailments. Mr. Sugrue declared that after her restoration to health she was adjudged by those who saw her to be about forty. Another woman achieved excellent results under an occult system of metaphysics, and guesses as to her age were fifteen years under her real age. He told also of a retired missionary who for the past twelve years had experimented with psychic phenomena and had obtained most startling results.

We can come to only one conclusion, and that is that all the systems, creeds, and cults work as a result of the firm beliefs of the individual—and that brings us to the magic of believing.

Sigmund Freud, the famous Austrian psychoanalyst, whose works are today standard for psychiatrists, brought the world's attention to the hypothesis that there was a powerful force within us, an unilluminated part of the mind—separate from the conscious mind—that is constantly at work molding our thoughts, feelings, and actions. Others have called this division of our mental existence, the soul, and some metaphysical teachers claim that it is located in the solar plexus. Others call it the super-ego, the inner power, the super-consciousness, the unconscious, the subconscious, and various other names. It isn't an organ or so-called physical matter, such as we know the brain to be, and science hasn't located its tangible position in the human body. Nevertheless, it is there, and from the beginning of recorded time man has known that it exists. The ancients often referred to it as the "spirit." Paracelsus called it the will, others have called it the mind, an adjunct of the brain. Some have referred to it as conscience, the creator of the "still, small voice within." Still others have called it intelligence and have asserted that it is a part of the Supreme Intelligence, to which we are all linked. Hence the name Universal Mind—that which embraces every living thing, all human as well as plant and animal life.

No matter what we call it—the writer prefers the word *subconscious*—it is recognized as the essence of life, and the limits of its power are unknown. It never sleeps. It comes to our support in times of great trouble, it warns us of impending danger, often it aids us to do that which seems impossible. It guides us in many ways and when properly employed performs so-called miracles.

Objectively, it does as it is told, that is, when it is commanded or besought by the conscious mind; subjectively, it acts primarily upon its own initiative, or appears to, although there are times when its activity appears to be the result of influences from the outside.

Sir Arthur Eddington is quoted as saying: "I believe that the mind has the power to affect groups of atoms and even tamper with the odds of atomic behavior, and that even the course of the world is not predetermined by physical laws but may be altered by the uncaused volition of human beings."

When this idea is fully comprehended, it becomes breath-taking. It is more understandable in the light of the electronic or vibratory theory.

Every student of the subject knows what may be accomplished by getting into direct contact with the subconscious mind—thousands have employed it to achieve wealth, power, and fame in this world, as well as to cure physical ailments and solve countless human problems. And its power is there for you to use. The only steps you have to take are to believe in its power and to use the technique set forth in this book, or else to devise a system of your own that will put it to work for you.

The late Dana Sleeth, whose syndicated column covering the observations of a hillbilly was well known to newspaper readers twenty years ago, once told me that he considered the subconscious mind one of his greatest aids not only in furnishing him with ideas but in assisting him to find lost tools and other articles. Mr. Sleeth at the time was living in the hills remote from cities and towns, alternating as a columnist and farmer. He had made an extensive study of the subject and we often discussed it as well as exchanged letters covering our ideas.

It's a wonderful thing—the subconscious mind [said Mr. Sleeth], and for the life of me I can't see why more people don't learn about it and its use. I don't know how many thousands of times it has helped me with my problems. Ideas for feature stories have often come to me when I was engaged in such lowly tasks as stump grubbing. And as for locating lost tools—it's a knockout.

You know nothing is ever lost—it's just misplaced. It's right there to be found in the exact place where you left it or dropped it. I have found dozens of misplaced tools in the identical spot where my subconscious mind told me to look. This is the way it would work. Say for example it was a pocket knife—mine's a good-sized one

—that I had misplaced or dropped. I would say, "Pocket knife, where are you?" Then I would close my eyes for a moment or I might gaze off into space—the answer might not always come immediately, but when it did it would come in a flash, and I would be led right to the spot where lay the knife. It always seemed to work unfailingly—even to such things as axes, rakes, and other tools that I was constantly leaving around somewhere—you know we newspaper people are not very methodical.

I used to have a great deal of difficulty in remembering names, but I have found that if I could visualize the man or woman whose name I had temporarily forgotten, and see an outline of his or her features, the color of the eyes, hair, manner of dress, etc., the subconscious would bring me the name without difficulty.

I don't know where I learned this but in trying to recall something, a certain story or certain fact that appeared at the moment to escape me, I would relax, elevate my head, put my right hand a couple of inches above my forehead, sometimes I might close my eyes or gaze off into space; but this little trick always seemed to get results.

Never forget: inventions, great musical compositions, poetry, fiction, and all other ideas for original accomplishment, come from the subconscious. Give it the thought or the material and keep it going with a deep-rooted desire for performance and you will get results. There is an old saying that once we start weaving, the Gods will furnish the skein, and how true that is.

When you start to operate with the aid of this power the bricks automatically fall into place as though a magical hand had touched them. Results will certainly follow in a most astounding manner. Ideas for accomplishment will pop here and they will pop there.

What may appear as coincidences are not coincidences at all but simply the working out of the pattern which you started with your own weaving.

I am certain that thousands of successful men and women reach great heights and accomplish marvelous results without knowing anything about the subconscious mind and with no knowledge that it was the power which made for accomplishments.

Living here in the hills away from people and everyday influences, I have often felt that those who live close to nature were in a much better position to utilize the subconscious than others. I believe that day will come when science will prove that the great power of the subconscious is one of the most formidable forces in shaping and controlling our lives.

A passing or momentary thought-flicker dies almost a-borning, although it may later reveal cumulative power. But the force that brings into play the great system of the subconscious is a sustained thought or, as previously stated, a fixed mental picture. There are many methods for stepping up the tempo of the vibrations of conscious thought in order to bring into action the subconscious forces, although sometimes just a single utterance, a momentary glance accompanying a word or two traveling from one person to another, has brought the subconscious into immediate play. So have catastrophic danger, moments of great peril and times of great stress, when, alone or in the company of others, a person is suddenly confronted with the necessity for immediate action. It comes to the aid of those in the habit of making quick decisions almost instantaneously, and it comes into operation when you have cleared your conscious mind of its multitude of conflicting thoughts. "Going into the silence" is another way of expressing it.

Perhaps the most effective method of bringing the subconscious into practical action is through the process of making mental pictures—using the imagination—perfecting an image of the thing or situation as you would have it exist in physical form. This is usually referred to as visualization.

However, most of the sustained and continuing manifestations come as a result of belief. It is through this belief with its strange power that miracles happen and that peculiar phenomena occur for which there appears to be no known explanation. I refer now to deep-seated belief—a firm and positive conviction that goes through every fibre of your being—when you believe it "heart and soul," as the saying goes. Call it a phase of emotion, a spiritual force, a type of electrical vibration—anything you please, but that's the force that brings outstanding results, sets the law of attraction into operation, and enables sustained thought to correlate with its object. This belief changes the tempo of the mind or thought-frequency, and, like a huge magnet, draws the subconscious forces into play, changing your whole aura and affecting everything about you—and often people and objects at great distances. It brings into your individual sphere of life results that are sometimes startling—often results you never dreamed possible.

There are countless references to it in the Bible. It is the first condition for membership in many religious, fraternal, and political organizations. Everywhere men are looking for people who have the kind of belief they will fight for, because it is the people who are charged with the vibrations of strong beliefs that sometimes do the miraculous, the things we so often say are "unbelievable." That kind of belief has the magic touch. It is also the basic principle in both white and black magic.

CHAPTER III

What the Subconscious Is

"THERE IS no artist, man of science, or writer of any distinction, however little disposed to self-analysis, who is not aware by personal experience of the unequalled importance of the subconscious," wrote Gustave Geley, distinguished French psychologist and author of *From the Unconscious to the Conscious*. He said also that the best results in life were obtained by close harmony and co-operation between the conscious and subconscious minds, and he pointed out that up to the nineteenth century the psychology of the subconscious was completely ignored, and it was then considered only as the abnormal outcome of disease or accident.

As the subconscious plays a very important part in the

magic of believing, it will bring you to a quicker understanding of this science if you have a clear and detailed
picture of what the subconscious mind is, where it is located,
and how it functions, both by itself and in collaboration with
the conscious mind. Some of the material in this chapter you
will find referred to or even repeated in succeeding chapters;
but as repetition is an essential part of the technique of this
science, it will be equally effective in presenting the knowledge of the science itself; and furthermore, the quicker you
get an understanding of it, the quicker you will be on your
way to getting what you desire.

In giving you this picture of the subconscious mind, it is
necessary for me to use scientific terms here and there, for
practically all the knowledge of the subconscious has come as
a result of the study and experimentation of some of the
world's greatest psychologists. But even if you find it a little
difficult to understand at first reading, repeated readings will
make it clear and you will thus have a solid foundation upon
which to proceed with the active part of the science.

In the first chapter I told you that it was *The Law of
Psychic Phenomena* by Thomson Jay Hudson that first got me
to thinking about the subconscious mind and its great possibilities for helping individuals in their everyday life. Since that
time there have been other books, such as *The Sub-Conscious
Speaks* by Erna Ferrell Grabe and Paul C. Ferrell, *The
Source of Power* by Theodore Clinton Foote, *The Unconscious* by Morton Prince, M.D., and *Common Sense and Its
Cultivation* by Hanbury Hankin, which have greatly added to
the knowledge of the subject. It will be my aim to give you
not only a mental picture of the conscious and subconscious
minds in the light of modern findings concerning their rela-
tions and functions, but also definite instructions as to the
method by which you can bring them under your control and
direct their energies toward assisting you to fulfill your desires.

"There is dormant in each human being a faculty, whether
it is developed or not, which will enable that particular
individual to succeed if the *desire for success* is present in his
conscious mind." Thus wrote the authors of *The Sub-Conscious Speaks*. This "faculty" has always been known and
recognized for its strange and unusual powers, but it was not

until about a century and a half ago that psychologists who made it the subject of their special investigation and experimentation, called it the subconscious mind. Emerson was certainly aware of the dual character of the human mental organization when he wrote in his *Journals:* "I find one state of mind does not remember or conceive of another state. Thus I have written within a twelve-month verses ('Days') which I do not remember the composition or correction of, and could not write the like today, and have only for proof of their being mine, various external evidences, as the MS. in which I find them, and the circumstances that I have sent copies of them to friends, etc., etc."

Today the words conscious and subconscious are widely understood, and it is recognized that we all have two minds, each one endowed with separate and distinct attributes and powers, and each one capable, under certain conditions, of independent action. There is no difficulty in your comprehending that the conscious mind operates in the brain, for whenever you do any concentrated thinking you feel it in your head. Sometimes the thought is so intense and prolonged that your head aches, or your eyes become tired, or your temples throb. Also, you can generally trace the source of the thought. It may be suggested by something you have seen or heard or read; perhaps it is a new idea for your business or your home; maybe it is the continuation of some thought you have been pondering for a long time past. The point is that you can connect it with something already related to your consciousness. Sometimes your thought is concerned with trying to solve a difficult problem, and you have become so exhausted and so discouraged at failing to arrive at the solution that you "give it up," "let the whole thing go," "dismiss it from your mind," a state of feeling you often have at night when you can't sleep because of the thought that is pounding and gripping your brain. The moment you "let it go," it begins to sink, as though it were moving downward somewhere inside of you. The tension in your conscious mind then decreases and you are soon asleep. The next morning when you wake up, your conscious mind begins to think again about the problem, when suddenly there appears before your mind's eyes a mental picture of your problem—completely solved and with all the necessary directions for appropriate action on your part.

Where did the thought go when you released it from your conscious mind and through what power inside of you was the problem solved? It is well known that many writers, orators, artists, musical composers, designers, inventors, and other creative workers have long made use of their subconscious minds either consciously or unconsciously. In this connection Merton S. Yewdale, well-known book publisher's editor, called the writer's attention to a recent statement by Louis Bromfield, the American novelist. Mr. Bromfield was quoted as saying:

> One of the most helpful discoveries I made long ago in common with some other writers is that there is a part of the mind, which the psychologists call the "subconscious," that works while you are sleeping or even while you are relaxing or engaged in some other task far removed from writing. I have found it possible to train this part of the mind to do a pretty organized job. Very often I have awakened in the morning to find a problem of technique, or plot, or character, which had long been troubling me, completely solved while I had been sleeping. The judgment of the "subconscious mind," which represents inherited instincts and the accumulation of experience, is virtually infallible, and I would always trust its decisions over any judgment arrived at through a long and reasonable process of conscious thinking.

No doubt you already have a mental picture of your two minds: the conscious mind in your head, above the line of consciousness; and the subconscious mind in your body, below the line of consciousness—with a means of communication between them.

Now it is the conscious mind that is the source of thought. Also, it is the mind that gives us the sense of awareness in our normal waking life: the knowledge that we are ourselves here and now: the recognition and understanding of our environment: the power to rule over our mental faculties, to recall the events of our past life, and to comprehend our emotions and their significance. More concretely, it enables us to have a rational understanding of the objects and persons about us, of our own successes or shortcomings, of the validity of an argument, or the beauty of a work of art.

The chief powers of the conscious mind are reason, logic, form, judgment, calculation, conscience, and the moral sense. By it we take cognizance of the objective world, and its means of observation are our five physical senses. Our conscious mind is the outgrowth of our physical necessities and likewise our guide in the struggle with our material environment. Its highest function is that of reasoning, and by all methods— inductive and deductive, analytic and synthetic. For example, suppose you are undertaking to discover a new serum. You use your conscious mind and employ the inductive method of reasoning. That is, you first collect the facts and elements that are presented to your sense perceptions; then you compare them one with another, noting similarities and dissimilarities; then you select those which are alike in qualities, in uses, or in function, after which you proceed to form a generalization or law, that certain things which have such qualities will function in such a way. This is the scientific method of arriving at knowledge, and it forms the basis of modern education in schools and colleges. But in some form or other we all use it to help solve our problems, whether personal, social, business, professional, or economic. Many times the solution of our problem results from this use of our conscious mind. But now and then when the solution is not forthcoming, we become exhausted with continued trying, we begin to lose confidence in ourselves, and we often resign ourselves to the idea that we have failed and that nothing can be done about it. Here is where the subconscious mind comes in—to help us to renew our belief in ourselves, to assist us to overcome our difficulty, and to put us on the road to achievement and success.

Just as the conscious mind is the source of thought, so the subconscious is the source of power. Also, it is one of the greatest realities in human life. It is rooted in instinct, and is aware of the most elemental desires of the individual, yet it is always pressing upward into conscious existence. It is a repository of spontaneous impressions of men and nature, and a memory vault in which are kept the records of facts and experiences that are sent down to it from time to time by the conscious mind for safekeeping and future use. Thus the subconscious mind is not only a mighty storehouse of ever-ready material which can be placed at the disposal of the conscious mind, but also a powerhouse of energy with which the individual can be charged, thus enabling him to recover his strength and courage, and also his faith in himself.

The subconscious mind is beyond space and time, and it is fundamentally a powerful sending and receiving station with a universal hookup whereby it can communicate with the physical, mental, psychic, and, according to many investigators, spiritual worlds, past, present, and future, as well. Such is the power of your subconscious mind. In brief, the subconscious embodies the feeling and wisdom of the past, the awareness and knowledge of the present, and the thought and vision of the future. Emerson, though he wrote of instinct, endowed it with so many superior attributes that he undoubtedly was thinking of the subconscious mind when he wrote: "All true wisdom of thought and of action comes of deference to this instinct, patience with its delays. To make a practical use of this instinct in every part of life constitutes true wisdom, and we must form the habit of preferring in all cases its guidance, which is given as it is used."

The powers of the subconscious are many, the chief of which are intuition, emotion, certitude, inspiration, suggestion, deduction, imagination, organization, and, of course, memory and dynamic energy. It takes cognizance of its environment by means independent of the physical senses. It perceives by intuition. It operates most successfully and performs its highest function when the objective senses are quiescent. But it can function during the waking hours as well as during sleep. It is a distinct entity, it possesses independent powers and functions, with a unique mental organization all its own, and it sustains an existence that is closely allied to the physical body and the life of the individual, and yet that also operates independently of the body.

Now the subconscious mind has three primary functions. First, with its intuitive understanding of the bodily needs, it maintains and preserves (unaided by the conscious mind) the well-being and indeed the very life of the body. Second, as pointed out in the previous chapter, in times of great emergency it springs into immediate action (again independently of the conscious mind) and takes supreme command, acting with incredible certitude, rapidity, accuracy, and understanding, in the saving of the life of the individual. Third, it is operative in the psychic world in which the psychic powers of the subconscious are manifested in such phenomena as telepathy, clairvoyance, and psychokinesis. But, also, it can be summoned to help the conscious mind in time of great personal necessity, when the conscious calls upon the subconscious to use its powers and resources to solve a vital problem or bring to pass that which is sought or desired by the individual.

In this book we are concerned particularly with the last part of the third primary function of the subconscious mind, and especially with the technique by which it operates for your benefit. Accordingly, to draw upon the resources and powers of the subconscious and awaken it into action, you must first be sure that you are asking for something that is rightfully yours to have and is within your ability to handle, for the subconscious manifests itself only according to the capabilities of the person. Then you must have patience and absolute faith, for, as Théodore Simon Jouffroy, the French philosopher, said, "The subconscious mind will not take the trouble to work for those who do not *believe* in it." Next, in conveying your need to the subconscious, it must be in the spirit—that the work has *already been done*. Thus, while it is necessary for you to *feel* and *think* yourself successful, it is important for you to go one step further and actually *see* yourself as already successful, either in the performance of some selected task or as actually occupying the position to which you are aspiring. For the next and final step, you must wait patiently while the subconscious is assimilating the elements of your problem and then goes about its own way to work it out for you.

In due course, with the flowing of the ideas and plans of the subconscious into your waiting conscious mind, the solution of your problem will be revealed to you and the correct course of action indicated, which you must follow immediately and unquestioningly. There must be no hesitation on your part, no mental reservation, no deliberation. You must receive the message from the subconscious freely, and after understanding it you must act on it at once. Only by so doing will you make your subconscious serve you and continue to respond whenever you call upon it.

However, your problem may be one that cannot be solved in the above manner; instead of receiving the solution in the form of a "blueprint," as it were, to guide your steps to the final fulfillment, you may, instead, feel some mysterious force urging you at intervals to do certain things that seem to have no special significance or logical connection. Nevertheless, you must continue to believe in the power and wisdom of the subconscious, and obediently perform the seemingly irrelevant things; one day you will find yourself in the position you sought through the aid of the subconscious, and doing the work you envisioned for yourself. Then, when you look back, you will see how the things you were called upon to do all formed a logical line of events, the last one of which was your final arriving—the reward of your sincerest hopes and desires —your own triumphant personal success!

CHAPTER IV

Suggestion Is Power

How MANY TIMES have you heard it said, "Just believe you can do it and you can!" Whatever the task, if it is begun with the belief that you can do it, it will be done perfectly. Often belief enables a person to do what others think is impossible. It is the act of believing that is the starting force or generating power that leads to accomplishment. "Come on, fellows, we can beat them," shouts someone in command, whether in a football game, on the battlefield, or in the strife of the business world. That sudden voicing of belief, challenging and electrifying, reverses the tide and—Victory! Success! From defeatism to victory—and all because some mighty believer knew that *it could be done*.

You may be shipwrecked or tossed into the water near a rocky shore, and momentarily you may fear that there isn't a chance for you. Suddenly a feeling comes that you *will* be saved or that you can save yourself. The moment you have that feeling it begins to take the form of belief, and along with the belief comes the power to assist you. You may be in a fire, surrounded by flames and enveloped in smoke, and frantic with fear. This same power asserts itself—and you may be saved. Emerson explains it by saying that in a difficult situation or a sudden emergency our spontaneous action is always the best. Many stories have been told of the great reserves of the subconscious mind, how under its direction and by imparting its superhuman strength frail men and women have been able to perform feats far beyond their normal powers. Great orators and writers are often amazed at the power of the subconscious mind to furnish them with a steady flow of thoughts.

After studying the various mystical religions and different teachings and systems of mind-stuff, one is impressed with the fact that they all have the same basic *modus operandi*, and that is through repetition—the repeating of certain mantras, words, formulas, or just plain mumbo-jumbo, which William Seabrook declared witch doctors, Voodoo high priests, "hexers," and many others followers of strange cults, use to invoke the spirits or work black magic. One finds the same principle at work in the chants, the incantations, litanies, daily lessons (to be repeated as frequently as possible during the week), the frequent praying of the Buddhists and Moslems alike, the affirmations of the Theosophists and the followers of Unity, the Absolute, Truth, New Thought, Divine Science; in fact, it is basic in all religions, although here it is white magic instead of black magic. When one seeks further, one sees the same principle at work in the beating of tom-toms or kettledrums by savages in all parts of the globe, the sound vibrations of which arouse similar vibrations in the psychic nature of these savages, so that they become stimulated, excited, and emotionalized to the point where they defy death. The war dances of the American Indians with their repeated rhythmic physical movements, the tribal ceremonies to bring rain, the dancing of the whirling dervishes, even the playing of martial music at critical times, as well as the spirited music that is played for the workers in many industrial plants, embody the same principle.

Some interesting facts as to the repetition of certain mystical chants and prayers are recounted by Theos Bernard in his book, *Penthouse of the Gods,* published in 1939. When he wrote it, he claimed to be the first white person to enter the mysterious city of Lhasa in Tibet, high in the Himalaya mountains, where dwell in monasteries thousands of lamas—followers of Buddha. On reading the book one gets the impression that when the lamas or monks are not eating or attending to the material wants of the body, they are constantly and continuously engaged in their mystical chants, using their prayer wheels. Bernard declared that in one temple the monks spent the entire day repeating prayers they had started at daybreak, the exact number of repetitions being 108,000. He told also of how lamas accompanying him repeated certain fixed chants for the purpose of giving him additional strength.

It is obvious that in all similar religions, cults, and orders there is a prescribed ritual in which the repetition of words, mystical or otherwise, plays an important part. And this brings us to the law of suggestion, through which all forces operating within its limits are capable of producing phenomenal results. That is, it is the power of suggestion—an autosuggestion (your own to yourself) or heterosuggestion (coming to you from outside sources)—that starts the machinery into operation or causes the subconscious mind to begin its creative work—and right here is where the affirmations and repetitions play their part. It's the repetition of the same chant, the same incantations, the same affirmations that leads to belief, and once that belief becomes a deep conviction, things begin to happen. A builder or contractor looks over a set of plans and specifications for a bridge or a building, and, urged by a desire to get the contract for the work, declares to himself: "I can do that. Yes, I can do that." He may repeat it silently to himself a thousand times without being conscious of doing it; nevertheless, the suggestion finds a place in which to take root, he gets the contract, and the structure is eventually built. Conversely, he may say that he can't do it—and he never does.

This is the identical force and the same mechanics that Hitler used in building up the German people to attack the world. A reading of his *Mein Kampf* will verify that. Dr.

René Fauvel, a famous French psychologist, explained it by saying that Hitler had a remarkable understanding of the law of suggestion and its different forms of application, and that it was with uncanny skill and masterly showmanship that he mobilized every instrument of propaganda in his mighty campaign of suggestion. Hitler openly stated that the psychology of suggestion was a terrible weapon in the hands of anyone who knew how to use it. Let's see how he worked it to make the Germans believe what he wanted them to and once that belief took hold, how they started their campaign of terror. Slogans, posters, huge signs, massed flags appeared throughout Germany. Hitler's picture was everywhere. "One Reich, one Folk, one Leader" became the chant. It was heard everywhere that a group gathered. "Today we own Germany, tomorrow the entire world," the marching song of the German youths, came from thousands of throats daily. Such slogans as "Germany has waited long enough," "Stand up, you are the aristocrats of the Third Reich," "Germany is behind Hitler to a man," and hundreds of others, bombarded them twenty-four hours a day from billboards, sides of buildings, the radio, and the press. Every time they moved, turned around, or spoke to one another, they got the idea that they were a superior race, and under the hypnotic influence of this belief, strengthened by repeated suggestion, they started out to prove it. Unfortunately for them, there were other nations who also had strong national beliefs that eventually became the means of bringing defeat to the Germans.

Mussolini, too, used the same law of suggestion in an attempt to make a place for Italy in the sun. Signs and slogans such as "Believe, Obey, Fight," "Italy must have its great place in the world," "We have some old scores and new scores to settle," covered the walls of thousands of buildings, and similar ideas were at the same time dinned into the people via the radio and every other means of direct communication by the spoken word.

Stalin, too, used the same science to build Russia into what she is today. The Institute of Modern Hypnotism in November, 1946, recognizing that Joseph Stalin had been using the great power of the repeated suggestion upon the Russian people in order to make them believe in their strength and power, named him as one of the ten persons with the "most hypnotic eyes in the world," rating him as a "mass hypnotist."

The Japanese war lords used it to make fanatical fighters out of their people. From the very day of their birth Japanese children were fed the suggestion that they were direct descendants of Heaven and destined to rule the world. They prayed it, chanted it and believed it; but here again it was used wrongly.

For forty-four years, ever since the Russo-Japanese war, the Japs immortalized Naval Warrant Officer Magoshichi Sugino, fabled as one of Japan's early suicide fighters and greatest heroes. Thousands of statues were erected to his memory and in repeated song and story young Nipponese were taught to believe that by following his example, they could die in no more heroic manner than as a suicide fighter. Millions of them believed it and during the war thousands of them did die as suicide fighters. Yet Sugino, who was supposed to have gone to his death while scuttling a ship to bottle up the Russian fleet at Port Arthur, didn't die. He was picked up by a Chinese boat, and upon learning that he was being lauded by his people as a great suicide fighter, decided to remain forever obscure and became an exile in Manchuria. Associated Press dispatches from Tokyo in November, 1946, tell how he was discovered after all these years and was being returned home. Although he was alive and well, it continued to be dinned into the ears of young Nipponese that there was no greater heroic act than to die as Sugino had. This terrible and persistent deeply founded belief, though based entirely on a fable, caused thousands of Japanese to throw away their lives during the war.

We, too, as Americans, were subjected to the power of suggestion long before and during World War I; we got it again in a big way under the direction of General Hugh Johnson with his N.R.A. plan, and in World War II it inspired us to increase our effort, to buy bonds, and so forth. We were constantly told that Germany and Japan had to be defeated unconditionally. Under the constant repetition of the same thought all individual thinking was paralyzed and the mass mind became grooved to a certain pattern—*win the war unconditionally*. As one writer said: "In war the voice of dissension becomes the voice of treason." So again we see the terrific force of thought repetition—it is our master and we do as we are ordered.

This subtle force of the repeated suggestion overcomes our reason, acting directly on our emotions and our feelings, and finally penetrating to the very depths of our subconscious minds. It is the basic principle of all successful advertising— the continued and repeated suggestion that first makes you believe after which you are eager to buy. In recent years we have enjoyed a vitamin spree. Vitamins for this and vitamins for that have come to us from all sides, and millions buy them in capsule form, so potent is the repeated suggestion of their value.

For centuries tomatoes were looked upon as poisonous. People dared not eat them until some fearless person tried them and lived. Today millions of people eat them, not knowing that less than a hundred years ago they were considered unfit for human consumption. Conversely, the lowly spinach may go into the discard, because our own United States Government declares that it does not contain the food values attributed to it for centuries. It is easy to see that millions will believe this and refuse any longer to honor Popeye's favorite dish.

Nothing is clearer than that the founders of all great religious movements knew much about the power of the repeated suggestion and with it gained far-reaching results. Religious teachings have been hammered into us from the time of our birth, into our mothers and fathers before us and into their parents and their parents before them, and likewise back through the centuries. There's certainly white magic in that kind of believing.

Such statements as "What we do not know will not hurt us" and "Ignorance is bliss" take on greater significance when we realize that the only things that can harm us or bother us are those of which we become conscious. We have all heard the story of the man who didn't know it couldn't be done and went ahead and did it. Psychologists tell us that as babies we have only two fears: the fear of loud noises and the fear of falling. All of our fears come with knowledge or develop as a result of our experiences; they come from what we are taught or what we hear and see. I like to think of men and women who, like staunch oak trees, can stand firm amid the many crosscurrents of thought that whirl around them. But far too many people are like saplings that are swayed by every little breeze and ultimately grow in the direction of some strong wind of thought that blows against them.

The Bible is filled with examples of the power of thought and suggestion. Read Genesis, chapter 30, verses 36 to 43, and you'll learn that even Jacob knew their power. The Bible tells how he developed spotted and speckled cattle, sheep, and goats by placing rods from trees, partially stripping them of their bark so they would appear spotted and marked, in the watering troughs where the animals came to drink. As you may have guessed, the flocks conceived before the spotted rods and brought forth cattle, "ringstraked, speckled, and spotted," and incidentally Jacob waxed exceedingly rich.

Moses, too, was a master at suggestion. For forty years he used it on the Israelites, and it took them to the promised land of milk and honey. David, following the suggestive forces operating on him, slew the mighty, heavily armed Goliath with a pebble from a slingshot.

The frail little Maid of Orléans, Joan of Arc, heard voices (?), and under their suggestive influences became imbued with the idea that she had a mission to save France. She was able to transmit her indomitable spirit to the hearts of her soldiers and she defeated the superior forces of the British at Orléans.

William James, father of modern psychology in America, declared that often our faith [belief] in advance of a doubtful undertaking is the only thing that can assure its successful conclusion. Man's faith, according to James, acts on the powers above him as a claim and creates its own verification. In other words, the thought becomes literally father to the fact. For further illumination of faith and its power, I suggest that you read the General Epistle of James in the New Testament.

Let us go into the field of sports where everyone who has ever witnessed a football or baseball game has actually seen this power of suggestion at work. The late Knute Rockne, famous coach at Notre Dame, knew the value of suggestion and used it repeatedly. But he always suited his method of applying it to the temperament of the individual team. A story is told that on one Saturday afternoon Notre Dame was playing in a particularly grueling game, and at the end of the first half was trailing badly. The players were in their dressing room nervously awaiting the arrival of Rockne. Finally the door opened and Rockne's head came in slowly. His eyes swept inquiringly over the squad—"Oh, excuse me, I made a mistake. I thought these were the quarters of the Notre Dame team." The door closed and Rockne was gone. . . . Puzzled and then stung with fury, the team went out for the second half—and won the game.

Others writers, too, have explained the psychological methods used by Rockne and have told how the late Fielding Yost of Michigan, Dan McGugin of Vanderbilt, Herbert Crisler of Princeton, and dozens of others, used the "magic" of suggestion to arouse their teams to great emotional heights.

Before the Rose Bowl game of 1934, the "wise" tipsters rated the Columbia team as "underdogs." They reckoned without Coach Lou Little and his stirring talks to his players day after day. The game started and everyone knew that Columbia "was in there." When the whistle blew for the end of the game, the Columbia men were the top dogs over the "superior" Stanford team.

In 1935 Gonzaga University beat powerful Washington State 13 to 6 in one of the most upsetting games ever seen in the West. Gonzaga was a non-conference team, while the Washington State team, because of its great record, was thought to be unbeatable. Newspaper stories at the time reported Sam Dagley, assistant coach, as having declared that Gonzaga played inspired football, and he revealed that Coach Mike Pecarovich for half an hour before the game played "over and over" a phonograph record of one of Rockne's most rousing pep talks.

Mickey Cochrane of the Detroit Tigers a number of years ago literally drove a second-division-minded group of baseball players to the top of the American League by using the same power of the repeated suggestion. I quote from a newspaper dispatch: "Day after day, through the hot, hard grind, he [Cochrane] preached the gospel of victory, impressing on the Tigers the 'continued thought' that the team which wins must go forward."

You see the same force actively at work in the fluctuations of the stock market. Unfavorable news immediately depresses prices, while favorable news raises them. Intrinsic values of stocks are not changed, but there is an immediate change in the thinking of the market operators, which is reflected at once in the minds of the holders. It is not what will actually happen, but what security holders believe will happen that causes them to buy or sell.

In the depression years—and there may be years like them in the future—we saw this same suggestive force working overtime. Day after day we heard the expressions, "Times are hard," "Business is poor," "The banks are failing," "Prosperity hasn't a chance," and wild stories about business failures on every hand, until they became the national chant, and millions believed that prosperous days would never return. Hundreds, yes thousands, of strong-willed men go down under the constant hammering, the continuous tap, tapping of the same fear vibratory thoughts. Money, always sensitive, runs to cover when fear suggestions begin to circulate, and business failures and unemployment follow quickly. We hear thousands of stories of bank failures, huge concerns going to the wall, etc., and people believe them readily and act accordingly.

There will never be another business depression if people generally realize that it is with their own fear thoughts that they literally create hard times. They think hard times, and hard times follow. So it is with wars. When peoples of the world stop thinking depressions and wars, they will become non-existent, for nothing comes into our economic scheme unless we first create it with our emotionalized thinking.

Dr. Walter Dill Scott, eminent psychologist and long president of Northwestern University, told the whole story when he said: "Success or failure in business is caused more by mental attitudes even than by mental capacities."

Human beings are human beings the world over, all subject to the same emotions, the same influences, and the same vibrations, and what is a big business, a village, a city, a nation but merely a collection of individual humans controlling and operating it with their thinking and believing? As individuals think and believe, so they are. As a whole city of them thinks, so it is; and as a nation of them think, so it is. This is an inescapable conclusion. Every person is the creation of himself, the image of his own thinking and believing. As

King Solomon put it, "For as he thinketh in his heart, so *is* he."

Recall the panic on the night of October 20, 1938, when Orson Welles and his Mercury Theater players put on the air a dramatization of H. G. Wells' novel, *The War of the Worlds*. It was a story of an invasion by some strange warriors from the planet Mars, but it caused fright among millions of people. Some rushed out-of-doors, police stations were besieged, eastern telephone exchanges were blocked. New Jersey highways were clogged. In fact, for a few hours following the broadcast, there was genuine panic among millions of listeners because they believed our earth was being attacked by invaders from Mars. Yes, indeed, belief can and does cause some strange and unusual happenings.

Rallies held in schools and colleges just before important athletic contests are based on the same principles—speeches, songs, and yells become the means of creating suggestion and arousing the will to win. Many sales managers employ the same principle in their morning sales meetings when frequently music from an orchestra, radio, or phonograph is used to emotionalize the salesmen and to get the idea over to them that they *can* beat all their previous sales records. The same principle with varying technique is basic in the army—in fact, in all armies. The commands and formations constantly repeated in close-order drill develop in the men instant obedience, which ultimately becomes instinctive; the commands and formations become so fixed in their minds and bodies that their movements are almost automatic—all of which in turn creates that self-confidence which is absolutely necessary in active conflict.

It is very important to remember that while the subconscious will get into action at once under the impetus of the commands or suggestions which it receives from the conscious mind, or which come from outside sources and are transmitted to it via the conscious mind, it gets results quicker if the conscious mind accompanies its message with a mental picture of the desired goal. It may be faint, sketchy, or even unfinished, but even if it is only an outline, it will be sufficient for the subconscious to act upon.

And this brings us to rituals and ceremonies which are performed amid dramatic settings in churches and secret orders, all designed to appeal to the emotions and to create a mystical picture in the minds of the beholders. These rituals, no matter what the setting, are there to hold your attention and to link the hidden meanings of these symbols with the particular ideas that are to be implanted in your mind. Various lighting arrangements, different paraphernalia, often a special garb for those directing the operations, all to the accompaniment of soft, often religious, music, help to create a mystical, or what some term a spooky, atmosphere in order to put you in the proper emotional, and incidentally receptive, state. The idea is as old as history. Not only the most civilized peoples but also the most primitive savage tribes have their characteristic ceremonials. Similar methods for impressing the individual are employed at mediumistic séances and crystal-gazing performances; even the gypsy phrenologist considers it a part of her "props." Without this atmosphere, which tends to make our conscious mind drowsy and even temporarily puts it to sleep, we would not be so easily convinced, for the desire to satisfy completely our longings for the mystical and miraculous is often not sufficient by itself to permit conviction.

This is not said with any idea of being sacrilegious, but to present a picture of the historic method of appealing to the masses, and to point out how awakening and stirring their emotional interest prepares the way to approach their reasoning mind. Appeal by drama is the first step in arousing the emotions of the people, no matter for what purpose.

Could the late Aimee Semple McPherson, she with the long flowing white robe and picturesque auburn hair-do, have put over her great act of saving souls as well as achieving healings, without her superb understanding of the power of the dramatic? It's something to wonder about, because Billy Sunday in his best table-sliding act was a novice compared to Aimee when it came to showmanship or a matter of plain impressiveness. She with her many artifices and stage settings put on a most solemn performance, and her followers, on the Pacific Coast at least, declare that the results she got were real and lasting. This is no reflection on the memory of Mrs. McPherson, for her followers were very sincere and believed in her work, her teachings, and the results—and that's all that matters.

However, there are men and women with strong personal magnetism, and great orators, who can get the same emotional effect without "props" or stage setting to aid them. They are masters of tone effects, emotional appeal, gesticulations, bodily movements, eye magnetism, etc., by which your attention is held and you yourself are thrown wide open to their driving appeal.

Let's consider charms, talismans, amulets, good-luck pieces, four-leaf clovers, old horseshoes, a rabbit's foot, and countless other trinkets which thousands of people believe in. By themselves, they are inanimate harmless objects without power, but when people breathe life into them by their thinking they do have power, even though the power isn't in them *per se*. The power comes only with the believing—which alone makes them effective.

Two outstanding illustrations of this are found in the stories of Alexander the Great and Napoleon. In Alexander's day, an oracle proclaimed that whoever unloosened the Gordian knot would become ruler of all Asia. Alexander, as you may remember, with one stroke of his sword cut the knot—and rose to tremendous heights and power. Napoleon was given a star sapphire when a child, with the prophecy that it would bring him luck and some day make him Emperor of France. Could it have been anything but the supreme belief in the prophecy that carried these two great men to a place in the hall of fame? They became supermen because they had supernormal beliefs.

A cracked or broken mirror isn't going to bring you bad luck unless you believe in it, and as long as the belief is fertilized, nurtured, and made a part of your inner self, it's going to bring you bad luck—believe it or not, because the subconscious mind always brings to reality what it is led to believe. One of our presidential candidates of a few years back, a man of high attainment and regarded by many as a man of great intelligence, was pictured as standing before the door of his barn above which was nailed an old good-luck horseshoe. The story goes that it was upside down. He was defeated. However, I mention this chiefly to show that beliefs in charms and symbols are not confined to simple, naturally superstitious people, but are frequently held by even the most enlightened.

It is claimed that there are people with certain mind powers which, when directed at plant life, such as grain, vegetables, flowers, and trees, can make them grow more abundantly. A number of years ago we had an old Swiss gardener who insisted that we replace in our yard a number of small trees and shrubs. At first I couldn't see the reason for digging up the old ones and replanting others, but the old man's insistence prevailed. I observed that in planting them, just after he got the small trees in the soil and covered the roots, he engaged in some sort of audible Mumbo Jumbo. He did the same with the shrubs. One day, my curiosity piqued, I asked him what he was "mumbling about" as he placed the trees and shrubs in the ground. He looked at me searchingly for a moment, then said: "You may not understand, but I'm talking to them, telling them they must live and bloom. It's something I learned when I was a boy from my teacher in the old country, Switzerland. Anything that grows should have encouragement and I'm giving it to them."

It is a long way from Switzerland to British Columbia, but in that Canadian province is a tribe of Indians, the members of which always talk to their halibut and salmon lines, hooks, and so forth, before actually starting to fish, claiming that if they didn't, the fish wouldn't bite. Many are the tales of South Sea Islanders who offer food to their tools and implements, talking to them as though they were alive, and beseeching them to get results. It isn't a great jump from those customs to the blessings offered at ship launchings or at sailing times of large fishing fleets in all civilized countries even today, where prayers are offered for successful voyages or ventures.

Observers have often declared that there appears to be a kind of affinity between certain humans and plants, which the plants seem to feel. There are thousands of professional gardeners who will plant seeds only at certain times of the moon. Superstition, you say? Perhaps it is practical mysticism. The Yale investigators referred to previously have also concluded that electrical fields play a major part in plant life, and certainly that is scientific.

When I think of those who plant only at certain times of the moon, I recall a thrifty neighbor of mine who, although a man of intelligence and mature years, had his hair cut at only certain times of the moon. I don't remember whether it was when the moon was waxing or waning that he would visit the barber, but whatever the phase of the moon, the time he selected, he maintained, caused his hair to grow less abundantly than if he had it cut at other times. I asked him once where he got such an idea and he glared at me as though I were belittling his intelligence. I never did get an answer to my question.

What has been said about plant and animal life may cause a lot of materialistic people to take violent issue, but it must be remembered that there are many forces at work in the world of which we know little or nothing. Consider how many new principles were developed in World War II. As this is written, the American Rocket Society has made application to the United States Government for land on the moon. Perhaps the application was made in a spirit of facetiousness, but who knows when some "Buck Rogers" will pilot a rocket plane to the moon? I, for one, wouldn't say it couldn't be done some day, for I don't know and neither do those who say it is impossible.

Without question human imagination or visualization and concentration are the chief factors in developing the magnetic forces of the subconscious mind. You have often heard the statement, "Hold the picture," and that, of course, means holding the mental picture or vision. Here again is where suggestion—repeated suggestion—plays its part. For example, you would like a new home and your imagination goes to work. At first you have only a hazy idea of the kind of house you would like. Then, as you discuss it with other members of your family or ask questions of builders or look at illustrations of new houses, the picture becomes clearer and clearer, until you visualize the house in all its particulars. After that the subconscious mind goes to work to provide you with that house. It may come into manifestation in any number of ways. You may build it with your own hands, or it may come to you through purchase or from the actions of outsiders. Its manner of coming is of no great consequence.

The process is the same when you are after a better job or planning a vacation trip. You've got to see it in your mind's eye, see yourself as holding that job, or actually taking the trip. Some of our fears become realities through our imaginations, just as Job's did. Fortunately, many of them do not, if we hold the mental picture only temporarily, or at least not long enough to have it focused fully upon the screen of our subconscious. The Biblical warning, "Where there is no vision, the people perish," is a fundamental truth, whether it be considered individually or collectively. For without the mental picture of accomplishment, little is done. You want a better job? You'll get it when you give your subconscious mind a mental picture of yourself holding that job.

As I write this, I think of the many experiences related to me by those who have used this science during the years, and I want to give you some of the stories, for in them you may perhaps find clues to an even more effective use of the principles and the mechanics of applying them, which I am setting forth.

A friend got the idea of building a boat. He knew nothing about boat construction, but believed that with some simple instructions he could build one. So he went ahead. In the course of the construction he found that he needed an electric drill, but he didn't want to spend $75 or $80 for the kind he wanted, especially when it would be used only a few months. First, he tried renting a drill, but inasmuch as it could be used only at night and had to be returned early the next morning, he found such an arrangement very inconvenient.

Then he told me: "I got thinking one night that somewhere there was a drill for me and I would have it placed in my hands. The more I thought about it, the more I thought it possible. However, nothing happened for several days; then one evening a friend who owned a sizable garage—a man I hadn't seen for a couple of years—came to see me. He, too, was interested in boats, and hearing that I was building one, said he'd like to look it over. He saw me floundering around with the heavy half-inch drill I was using and asked me where I got it. I told him I had rented it and he laughed, saying, 'Come over to the shop tomorrow and I'll lend you a smaller one which you can handle much easier.' Needless to say, I got it and kept it during all the period I was constructing the boat.

"A somewhat similar experience happened when I was cutting the ribs. I had a small jig saw, but found that it wouldn't cut through three-quarter-inch lumber. Then I found myself wishing for a band saw—that thought led me to a place a few blocks away from my house where I knew there was a woodworking shop. I could use the band saw if I paid the owner fifty cents an hour for its use. However, I found that I was running to and from my home, first to fit the ribs and then to shape them, and losing too much time in the process. I frequently said to myself during those days that there was some easier way to get the use of a band saw, and there was.

"The following Sunday another friend came to see how the boat was getting along and when I told him that I had been slowed down without the use of a band saw, he too laughed, saying, 'I bought one Thursday and I will not be using it for some little time. Got to get my shop fixed up and in the meantime you're welcome to use it.' As a matter of fact, he delivered it to me that same day and I kept it a number of months. I finished the boat!"

Another man told me the story of how he got the use of a thirty-foot extension ladder with which to paint his house. "I thought I would undertake the painting in my spare time," he told me, "and began looking around to find where I could get the use of a ladder. I found places where I could rent one, but they fixed time requirements which didn't fit into my plans. I don't know how many times I said to myself: You're going to find a ladder. And I did. It was Memorial Day, and while in my back yard I happened to notice that a neighbor across the street from me was using a long ladder to wash off the walls of his house. I called to him, asking where he got the ladder. He told me he had bought it when he purchased the house. That afternoon it was in my back yard, and I had the loan of it for several weeks!"

Another man told me that shortly after the United States entered the war, he wanted a garbage can of a certain size, but because of priorities he was unable to locate what he wanted. He said he visited second-hand stores, junk-shops, bakeries, and garages, in an endeavor to find the kind of container he wanted, but without success. He was about to give up hope when one morning he noticed workmen who were making repairs on a concrete building across from his home. They were using some waterproofing material from a can, exactly the kind of can he had pictured for his own use. He said he asked the man in charge of the work what would be done with the container when the work was finished and he was told that it would be left on the ground to be hauled away. He then explained his wants, and a couple of days later the container was in his garage—the workmen had not only emptied it but had washed and scrubbed it before delivery!

I had taken my car to a shop owner for repairs to the ignition system, after several had failed to locate the trouble. I told him how the car had been acting, and after listening he said, "I believe I can fix it." I casually remarked, "Belief is a great thing, isn't it?"

"You bet it is. Thought is the greatest force in the world and the dumb ducks laugh when you talk about it," he answered rather caustically.

"I don't, I'm interested," I replied. "Tell me of some instances where you have demonstrated the power of thought."

"I could keep you here all day telling you of its power—at least in my own life."

"Tell me a few. When did you first become aware of it?"

"Oh, I guess about twelve years ago when I fell and broke my back. I was in a cast for a long time and the doctors told me that even if I recovered I would be crippled the rest of my life. As I lay on my back in the hospital worrying about my future, I frequently thought of the words used by my mother to the effect that 'One just has to believe.' One day it dawned on me that if I could hold on to the mental picture I was going to be all right, and if I believed in it sufficiently, I could get well. To make a long story short, here I am crawling over and underneath cars, and far from being a cripple as you can see for yourself."

"Very interesting. Tell me of more cases," I urged.

"Well, I've used it frequently to get more business. As a matter of fact, this present location is a result of it. As you know, I was burned out at my old place a few weeks ago and, owing to the war, space like this in the city is well-nigh impossible to find. For two or three days, worrying about my possible inability to get another location, I deliberated whether I should attempt to continue with the business or go to work for someone else. Then one night I made up my mind I would continue in business for myself. That was the turning point, and just before I went to sleep I said to myself, 'Oh, you'll find a place within the next few days. This thought power hasn't failed you yet.' I went to sleep with full confidence that the place would be forthcoming. The very next day I went over to see the painter where I had taken the car I saved from the fire, and mentioned that I was looking for another place. 'That's funny,' he commented, 'you can rent this space, for I've just bought the building in the next block from an owner who wanted to retire.' And here I am on a main thoroughfare and with more business than I can possibly handle!"

I know that some readers will say that these are merely coincidences, but my files are filled with similar "coincidences." To some of you they may be just that, but those who are acquainted with this science know that these things have come about as the result of intensified thought or mental picture-making. However, we come again to a matter of opinion—the difference in conclusions between those who think this is all nonsense and those who know that the things we think materialize after their kind.

Again we are reminded of what Paracelsus said: "Men who are devoid of the power of spiritual perception are unable to recognize anything that cannot be seen externally."

It is pretty well agreed that the subconscious mind works as a result of images thrown upon its screen, but if there is something wrong with your projection apparatus or the original slide, then the projected image is blurred, inverted, or a total blank. Doubts, fears, counterthoughts, all have a part in blurring the pictures you consciously desire to project.

Those who have well-developed imaginations, such as great artists, writers, and inventors, possess the ability to visualize or to make mental pictures almost at will. However, with the mechanics which will be enlarged upon later and the explanations already given, anyone following them should have no difficulty in being able to see in his mind's eye the things, objects, or situations as he desires them to be in reality.

One of the greatest fishermen I ever knew used this visualizing method. He could sit in a boat with one or two others and pull trout after trout out of the water, while his companions, using the same kind of bait or fly and with apparently the same mechanical technique, cast or dropped their flies or hooks in the same places repeatedly, but without results. I asked him about it one time and he laughingly replied: "I put the old 'squeeza-ma-jintum' [his word for magic] on them. I figuratively or mentally get down there where they are, and tell them to hook the bait or fly. In other words, I see them snapping at the hook and believe that it will work. That's all I can give you in the way of an explanation."

This story was told to another fisherman not blessed with the first fisherman's luck, and he scoffed at it. "Ridiculous," he declared. "Any good fisherman must know the stream, the holes, the habits of fish, the type of bait or flies to use, and he'll catch them if they are there." However, he couldn't explain how others skilled in fishing technique could fish in an identical spot and still not catch them like the man who used the old "squeeza-ma-jintum." The writer is not a fisherman, but surely if this law of attraction works in other ways, there is no reason why it could not be used advantageously in fishing.*

Now, let's go into the field of golf. For many years I was interested in the game and was a member of several clubs. I frequently played with a man who in his younger days had been one of the world's tennis champions. This man was one

---

*Ben Hur Lampman, associate editor of *The Oregonian,* author of many articles and books on fishing and kindred subjects, twice an O. Henry Memorial Award winner, and a recognized naturalist, upon reading the foregoing said:

"The man who says that it is ridiculous to consider your fishing friend as claiming there's some sort of magic or attraction at work when he catches fish when others fishing in the same spot get mediocre results, merely makes himself ridiculous by displaying his ignorance. I can't explain how your friend is always so fortunate in making his catches beyond saying that there is decidedly something psychic about successful fishing. Any one who has studied the habits of fish and tried to catch them sooner or later realizes that there is more to successful fishing than merely throwing a lure or bait into a place where the fish are supposed to be. Just what the relationship is between mind and fish—if any—I can not explain, but having been a student of fish, their ways and habits practically all my life, I do know that in successful fishing there is an unexplainable element or factor at work—call it what you please. I say it is something psychic and undoubtedly in the realm of psychic phenomena lies the explanation of the so-called fisherman's 'luck' or the 'squeeza-ma-jintum' or magic of your successful fisherman friend."

of the most amazing short-shot players on the Pacific Coast. With his mashie or mashie niblick he could place the ball on any desired spot on the green with a dead stop, as close to or as far from the pin as he desired, and he was usually down in one putt. His putting, too, was an art to marvel at.

"How did you do it, George?" I asked him one day when he amazed everyone in our foursome with what could be called phenomenal shots. "Well," he replied, "you've played handball and squash, and you know what it means to place your shots on the front wall. You intuitively place it high or low or so it will rebound to a side wall or result in a kill or an extremely low ball. I learned placement years ago in tennis. You have sort of a mental picture where you want the ball to go or land before you hit it with your racquet or hand. I use the same principle with my short shots and putting. In other words, when I face the green and before I swing my club, I have an instant mental picture of where I want the ball to land, and when I putt I actually see the ball dropping into the hole. Of course, a proper stance, knowledge of handling the clubs, and so forth, are vital. But most golfers have that and still don't get results. It is true that I spend many hours in practice, so do others; but the main thing is that I just seem to know where the ball is going to land before the club hits it. There's a confidence or a belief existing that I can do it and with a mashie or mashie niblick I cause a backspin that will bring the ball to a dead stop when it lands."

For you who may raise your eyebrows at this, let's examine the facts given in a newspaper story written by the famous sports writer, Grantland Rice. It appeared in the middle 'thirties and had to do with the phenomenal amateur golf player, John Montagu. Rice declared that Montagu could run rings around anyone and that the ball always landed where he wanted to place it, whether 300 yards down the fairways or a chip shot to within two or three feet of the cup, and then when he putted it was like the crack of doom. Rice said that the ball went where Montagu wanted it to go. Now let's read Montagu's own explanation as given in the same newspaper story. He said: "Golf to me is played with the head, mind or brain or whatever you wish to call it. Of course, there are fundamentals of stance, grip, swing; but I must have a clear, clean mental picture of what I am doing before I play the shot. That mental picture takes charge of the muscular reaction. If there is no mental picture—what happens is a mere guess. This means almost endless concentration of thought if you are under pressure and there is no thrill in any game unless you are under pressure."

Gene Sarazen, who was one of the greatest golf professionals of all times, used similar methods in his matches, and if you read his little book *Golf Tips,* you will find that he has much to say about mental pictures, objectives, concentration, and confidence. All golfers have heard of "mental hazards." In reality, they are bunkers, traps, water hazards, etc. But in the imaginations of many players they are formidable handicaps to put fear into the hearts of the players. On one course where the writer often played there was a water hole. The distance from the tee to the hole was about one hundred and twenty yards spanning a small pond approximately fifty feet wide, an easy shot with a mashie or a mashie niblick for the average player. One member of the club who had been a great baseball and football player in his younger days, for a long time could never get over this water hazard. Invariably with his irons he would put ball after ball into the water, to the accompaniment of profanity on his part and laughter on ours. Finally, as the months went by he took to using his spoon and hitting the ball far beyond the green. One day I said to him, "I know, the water fools you, but the next time just blot out of your mind the picture that there is water between the tee and the green and see instead, mentally, an easy short fairway before you." The first time he followed the suggestion his ball fell a few inches from the pin, and from that time on, he later told me, as long as he followed the blotting-out technique, he never had any trouble; but when he was unable to concentrate on his own mental picture, due to the joshing from other members of his foursome, he landed in difficulties.

In observing many pool and billiard games, I am convinced that certain skilled players influence the direction and fall of the balls by mind control, although they may be completely in ignorance of the power they are using. If it can work on a golf ball, it certainly can work on a billiard ball.

Roy Chapman Andrews tells the story of a San Antonio,

Texas, man, who with a twenty-two calibre rifle fired more than 14,500 shots at small blocks of wood tossed into the air without a single miss. Mr. Andrews emphasized perfect timing and remarkable accuracy. Nothing was said of the mind-pictures; but if you have ever done any prolonged trap or target shooting, you know the part visualizing plays.

One finds the same sort of "magic" at work in all fields of sports. Great baseball batters, expert forward-passers in foot-ball, accurate drop-kickers—all consciously or unconsciously picture connecting with the ball and placing it where they want it to go. Certainly, practice, timing, and so forth, all have their primary importance, but the mental side must never be overlooked.

In this connection, I was impressed by several statements made by Dr. Marcus Bach in his recent book, *They Have Found a Faith*. Dr. Bach tells of bowling with Father Divine, and of observing from the way Father Divine selected a ball, and from his stance and delivery, that he was no bowler. Yet Father Divine made a strike on his first try and, according to Dr. Bach, it was one of the prettiest strikes he ever saw. Dr. Bach says: "Father's nonchalance was characteristic. He rubbed the soft palms of his hands together as if to say, 'Well, what do you expect when the Lord rolls one!' "*

Again Dr. Bach speaks of an interview with Rickert Fill-more, manager of Unity City and son of one of the founders of the Unity movement, in which he asked if the works of Unity could be applied to a real estate venture. Mr. Fillmore replied, "If it works at all, it works everywhere."

Many readers of this book may not be golfers or billiard players, but here's a simple experiment that will demonstrate to you this strange power of attraction through visualizing or making the mental picture actually work. Find a few small stones or pebbles which you can easily throw and locate a tree or a post of six to ten inches in diameter. Stand away from it twenty-five or thirty feet or any convenient greater distance and start throwing the pebbles in an endeavor to hit it. If you are an average person, most of the stones will go wide of their

---

*From *They Have Found a Faith* by Marcus Bach, Copyright, 1946. Used by special permission of the Publishers, The Bobbs-Merrill Company.

mark. Now stop and tell yourself that you can hit the objective. Get a mental picture of the tree figuratively stepping forward to meet the missile or the stone actually colliding with the tree in the spot where you want it to strike, and you'll soon find yourself making a perfect score. Don't say it's impossible. Try it and you'll prove that it can be done—if you will only believe it.

In the early days of wartime gasoline rationing when most people didn't consider getting additional coupons a criminal offense, a friend found he didn't have enough gas to take him to his duck lake. One Sunday while in his home he told me how he had secured sufficient coupons to make several trips to the shooting grounds. Said he: "I had just about given up the idea of duck shooting this fall when the thought occurred to me that I could put this Mind Stuff to work and get some more gas. Of course, everyone around the office knew that I wanted to go duck shooting and most of them knew of my problem. Whether they passed out word to their friends I do not know, but I got more coupons than you could shake a stick at. I had a constant picture of going hunting and using my automobile and of someone giving me coupons. It may be hooey, but I got the gasoline coupons. Even a farmer friend gave me gas out of his allotment."

Now let's take this same science into the kitchen. Did it ever occur to you that the so-called good cooks use this same science, some consciously and others unconsciously? Two people can attempt to make the same kind of pie. Identical ingredients will be used and instructions followed to the letter—one will be a failure while the other will be the last word in culinary achievement. Why? In the first case, the one cook approaches pie-making with trepidation. She knows she has had pie failures in the past and wonders how this one is going to come out. She doesn't have a perfect mental picture of an appetite-satisfying golden brown crust with a wonderful zestful filling. She's upset and nervous, and, without her knowing it, her uneasiness is communicated to her pie-making. The second one knows that she knows that the pie is going to be "tops"—and it is. That primary mental picture—her belief—makes it so.

If you are a mediocre cook and you like to cook—that's a

very necessary requisite too—sell yourself on the idea that you can prepare superior dishes and you can do it, for you have the forces inside of you and they will come to your aid if you will only believe in them and call upon them. So put your heart and soul into the next pie you make and even you will be surprised at the result when you see the realization of your mental picture of the perfect pie.

The same law will work no matter where it is applied, and that goes for everything from fishing to money-making or success in business. Let's take an example out of the war. General Douglas MacArthur declared when he left the Philippines: "I shall return." With our Pacific Fleet in ruins at Pearl Harbor, practically no airplanes or transports at the time, and with the Japanese in control of most of the South Pacific, MacArthur had no physical evidence that he would ever return. However, he must have had a mental picture of his return or he would have never made the statement. It was a statement of confidence or belief, and history relates his triumphant return. Thousands of similar cases happened during the war and are happening today.

CHAPTER V

The Art of Mental Pictures

WHEN I WAS in the investment banking business, one of the salesmen, a young chap, came into my office for advice.

"I wish you would tell me how I can overcome my fear of ————. I know I can sell him if I can get in to see him and talk with him on his own level. As it stands, he's got the life scared out of me and every other salesman."

The man the salesman referred to is a millionaire with a very imposing office organization. He is a portly type, with a heavy shock of hair and beetle-browed; because of his growling manner, he easily scares timid folks. However, I knew he liked people who talked up to him.

The salesman had been picturing this man as he saw him and momentarily I was puzzled, but the answer soon came and I said: "You know he's not going to hurt you physically. Suppose you saw him at the beach in a bathing suit, you wouldn't be afraid of him there, would you, even though he did appear to be a pretty hairy fellow?"

"Certainly not," replied the salesman. Then the idea of a hairy body came to me and I asked the salesman: "Bob, did you ever see one of those clownish dancing bears, tied to a grind organ, wearing a fez or a dunce cap? You know they can growl, but most of them are toothless and can't bite."

"Sure," responded the salesman.

"Well, you have an imagination. Just picture our friend as one of those harmless old bears, fez, collar, and all, and the mental hazard is gone, isn't it?"

The salesman, laughing heartily, went out. A few days later he sold the man $20,000 worth of securities, and this executive may still be wondering how the young salesman ever got in to see him, to say nothing of selling him. At last accounts, the young fellow was still selling this wealthy man.

A couple of weeks later the same salesman was back in my office, telling me how he had used similar methods in making another sale, this time to a gruff old man who wore white whiskers, had a patriarchal and stern appearance, and used a vitriolic tongue that was feared by most salesmen.

"That old goat had me buffaloed for a long time. I knew he had money, but every time I passed his store and saw him scowling—he was always scowling—I couldn't get up courage to go in and tackle him. A few days ago I got thinking of the picture-making plan you told me to use on ———— and the idea popped into my head of a picture of Santa Claus. I said to myself, 'Sure, the old goat could be Santa Claus and who's afraid of that kindly old boy?' Well, it worked there too. The old man was swell to me—sort of flattered that a young fellow like me dared approach him. I got a $5000 order out of him and he told me to come back next week as he wanted to go over his whole security list with me. That means more business."

There are many men holding executive positions who assume an importance that causes some people to hold them in awe. With their elaborate office surroundings and their numerous secretaries and clerks, they put on a show that proves impressive to some people. Just bear in mind that these executives are mere human beings with the same fears, the same frailties, the same faults that are common to millions; at home they are often docile little souls. When you do this and picture them as they really are, rather than as they appear or pretend to be, the mental hazard immediately disappears. The genuinely great man is usually easy to approach and seldom barricades himself from callers. If you are a salesman, this should give you a clue to how to eliminate the mental hazards that crop up when you call upon someone who puts on a show of being superior.

A lawyer told me of an experience that nicely illustrates my point.

"I once found myself pitted against a lawyer who had a great reputation and was generally feared by young men. For a little while in the courtroom, I admit I was frightened, but I closed my eyes and said to myself, 'I'm just as good as he is; as a matter of fact, I'm better. I can lick him and I will.' I repeated words and phrases like that for several seconds and when I opened my eyes, I could have licked two like him. I now go through the same little ritual whenever I get a tough case or the jury doesn't look favorable. Maybe it's luck, maybe it's all illusory, but it always works."

People who act and appear hard-boiled are usually "softies" at heart and once an interviewer eliminates the mental hazard, he has licked the situation. Take a couple of deep breaths the next time you call on one, convince yourself he'll be a "push-over," and he will.

During the depression days of the 'thirties, a group of managers and assistant managers, including the butchers of a large grocery chain store, came on their initiative to me for help. After a six weeks' course of lectures, the men decided to put the lectures into effect. It was agreed that each store one day a week would use the science I had expounded to push the sale of certain items. After considerable debate, among the items selected for the test were cheese, rolled roasts, salmon, and just plain Hubbard squash. (The manager of a store in one of the outlying districts had said he could make a good buy of squash from a farmer customer.) The day before each sale the managers carefully coached their clerks to make a mental picture of each customer coming into their stores and buying the selected items. Of course, prominent displays were made of each item, and each clerk was instructed to think of selling the special item during the day whenever a customer appeared. The results were astounding. The store specializing in cheese sold more cheese in that one day than had passed over the counter in a six months' period; the shop which on Saturday specialized in the rolled roasts had them sold before noon; the store which on Friday had featured fresh salmon sold more salmon than all the other stores of the group combined; the one where squash had been selected had to call upon the farmer twice during the day to replenish the supply.

Today, with only one exception and he is a war casualty, each man who took the lecture course is either in business for himself or has a much better job. As a matter of fact, one of the men now owns three stores of his own, while another is manager of a chain of stores in a neighboring state.

I think of a recent conversation with the head of a large Pacific Coast advertising agency, who for a number of years handled the sales promotion work for a well-known coffee manufacturer who had recently sold his business.

"If there was ever a man who used this stuff to tremendous advantage," declared the advertising executive, "it was old man ————. He came to this section as a kid and learned the coffee roasting and blending business. He concluded that he could do better if he were in business for himself. He thoroughly believed that he could blend the best coffee, and even up to the time of his retirement, after years in the business, he thoroughly believed that his coffee was the best on the market. Of course, that belief made a millionaire of the old man."

Once I had given a printer a small manuscript that I wanted to get out in pamphlet form which dealt with the subject we are now considering. The next morning he popped into my office, almost out of breath and visibly shaking. Naturally, I asked if there were anything wrong, and he spluttered: "Just had the oddest experience. I took your manuscript home last night and read it, and I said to myself, 'If the stuff actually works as the author claims, then I ought to be able to find a parking space close to his office when I go to see him.' I thought no more about it until I was driving from our plant to your office just a few minutes ago, and then the thought again occurred to me that it might work. Well, I turned the corner and there wasn't a space to be seen on Sixth Avenue, and I was going to dismiss it all as bunk. But as I slowed down to let some pedestrians pass, I saw a machine pull away from the curb right in front of this building and there was my place. It gives me goose-pimples. Maybe it's just one of those things."

"Perhaps," I said, "but why not try it again?"

He did, and had similar results over a period of years. Call them coincidences if you like. But this printer never would, especially when shortly afterward he was able to more than treble his business while most printers were having a difficult time to get any orders.

Now and then I told acquaintances about the experiences of the printer and I was astounded to learn that others seemed able to find parking space as had this printer. One woman, a Unity student, told me that she and her sister never drove downtown without saying that they would find a parking space in or near a spot that they desired—and they always found it.

A woman, a dietician and instructor in a large hospital, said to me: "The working of this power, or whatever it is, often frightens me. As an illustration, this happens with continued frequency. Every morning on my way to work when I enter the business section, the traffic lights always turn green and I get through all of them without a stop. I cannot recall the time that the lights have shown red against me. Now I just take it all as a matter of course."

A few months ago a woman was arrested for violating the traffic signals, but according to the newspaper stories at the time, she convinced the judge that the green light was on when she crossed the intersection. She was a motherly woman and the judge freed her when she told him, "Judge, the light just had to be green, and it always is for me because I keep repeating as I near an intersection 'Green light be on, green light be on.' "

The police maintained, however, that there were no signals at this intersection—only the flashing intermittent red light. But here was the motherly old lady convincing the judge of her belief, and obviously she believed in her ability to have the signals the way she wanted them.

A woman told me of an automobile trip made from Washington, D.C., to join her husband who had been assigned to duty in a Pacific Coast city. "I was frightened in the beginning," she said. "I had never driven any such distance alone in my life. One day I got thinking of my grandmother who had been one of the pioneers to the Pacific Northwest and who had done many things alone. My fear was gone at once. However, the garage man who looked over my car before I started told me not to go without getting new tires; he said the old ones would blow out any time. If I hadn't been so intent on making the trip and without delay, I might have listened to him; but the thought again came to me that they would last until I got across the country—and last they did. While I do not use the car much now, the original tires are still there, though in pretty bad shape. But no blowouts ever occurred."

Another case that reinforces my contention involves an oil refining company and more than a million dollars of investors' money. In its early days the company experienced great financial difficulties brought on by suits and marketing problems, and it became necessary to reorganize the whole financial structure, with the security holders taking new securities but foregoing interest for a number of years. The stockholders were told to make a mental picture of the oil turning into money and coming from every still and every spigot—in short, to visualize the company as a money-maker. Incidentally, this company was in a field dominated by strongly intrenched major companies. Nevertheless, not only did the company become a substantial money-maker, but it was subsequently sold and all the security holders got back their money with interest in full.

Jimmy Gribbo, well known to sports fans as a manager of prizefighters, has made winners out of many boxers by teaching them how to visualize themselves as winners—and they became winners.

The writer is aware that some of his readers, especially those who know nothing about Mind Stuff, will question these stories but those who related them are of undoubted veracity, and the writer also thinks that there are many of his readers who from their own experiences could relate much stranger tales.

G. N. M. Tyrrell, a well-known English investigator and writer, declares that if while dwelling upon the activity of the subconscious mind we determine upon an intention to do a certain thing, we may subconsciously initiate a train of events likely to bring this thing about. The statement is credited to Dr. Shailer Mathews, long associated with the University of Chicago, "that we influence events by very great desires, and there is psychological proof on ourselves of the effects of our own desires."

Here are two cases directly in point.

The woman head of a large antique shop, a recognized authority on antiques whose advice concerning them was much sought after by other women, happened to dislike social activities. She was constantly bothered by a woman to accompany her to luncheons and teas. This second woman merely wanted to be seen in the company of this authority on antiques, and invitation after invitation had been declined by the authority. A well-known lecturer was scheduled to talk before a woman's club, and under the insistent pleas of the second woman the head of the antique shop finally agreed to go with her.

"She caught me in an off moment," she told me, "and no sooner had I agreed than I began to regret that I had made the promise to go. I hate those would-be highbrow affairs and this was going to be one, I was certain. Actually at night I would have cold sweats thinking about what I had done and how I could get out of going without offending the woman, who was a fairly good customer of the store, and who, incidentally, I knew would have a lot of mean things to say about me should I fail to keep my agreement.

"I thought about it and thought about it, figuring on making up excuse after excuse—none of which seemed good enough or plausible. I was nearly beside myself. The woman and I had nothing in common. As a matter of fact, she bored me. The day of the meeting was drawing near and I had about concluded to phone her, telling her that an important engagement had come up making it impossible to attend the lecture, when in she came.

"She was all apologies when she informed me that the

lecture had been canceled. Did I draw a sigh of relief? I thoroughly believe in what you preach and I think that my thought had something to do with what happened. I know that some will say it was a coincidence—let them call it that if they please. But stranger things than that happen, and they're not all coincidences."

The second story involves the manager of a company manufacturing a hay fever remedy. He had recently arrived in town, found an apartment near his office, and sought a telephone for his apartment. At that time, just after the war, the telephone company had a long waiting list and was installing telephones only on very high priorities, such as service for doctors, police, fire officials, and those engaged in public emergency work.

He had tried for two months, without success, to get a telephone, seeking out everyone he could to help him. Through a mutual friend he learned that I knew the manager of the company and he came to see me. I quickly disillusioned him of the idea that I could get the manager to give him a telephone ahead of several thousand others, but I did tell him that if he could establish his rights to a priority, he shouldn't have any trouble.

I asked him whom he had talked with and he gave me the names of several people occupying both major and minor positions with the company. Then he explained that it was imperative that he have a telephone, for he was the only one connected with his own company who could handle after-office-hour business.

"Do you have many long-distance calls?" I asked. "And how much does your company telephone business amount to a month?"

He gave me an unusually high figure for his monthly bills.

"Take your last few months' bills with you and see the man you saw first, look him straight in the eye and tell him that you've just got to have a telephone without delay," I told him, "but don't go near him until you can convince yourself that you can convince him. Otherwise, your task is futile. You've just got to make up your mind that you're going to have a telephone installed in your apartment, and you must believe it."

"I'll try it," he said, then quickly catching himself said, "No, I'll do it. I'll get that telephone."

He came to see me several days later.

"It certainly worked. I must tell you about this, for it's very funny how a positive thought brings about such a series of happenings. I went to see the man I had first talked with, and he was rather amazed that I had come back to him. I explained in detail this time why it was imperative that I have a phone, I showed him the bills as you suggested, and it was only a matter of minutes before I had him convinced. He was just about to call the manager to plead my cause when, lo and behold, the manager called him on some other matter. Then this man told the manager of my troubles and the manager agreed I was entitled to a priority. He suggested that I see a Mr. ———— in charge of priority ratings. I had never heard of this man before and prior to that time had known nothing of the priority system. I saw this man, told him my story and considerable about our business, referring to the product which we manufactured. I nearly collapsed when he told me that he was bothered by hay fever and had tried various remedies without results. It was a natural from then on. It all gives me a sort of spooky feeling. How did it happen that the manager called the man I was talking with at that particular time and how did it happen that the man with the final say-so was a hay fever victim and one I could help? From now on send me the scoffers."

Of course, we all know that our thoughts determine our carriage, our facial expression, our conversation, for what we are outwardly comes as the result of what we think habitually. There are many women who have improved their appearance by continuing to feel the delights of beauty, by thinking thoughts of the beautiful, by wearing stylish clothes, by adding things of beauty to their surroundings, by developing poise and easy carriage, and by constantly telling themselves that they are going to win out. You have seen in movie plays how a badly dressed, ordinary-looking girl can be transformed into a most attractive woman by beautiful clothes and the latest style of hair-do. You can do the same thing—and you will speed up the process if you will continue to hold the mental picture of your new self and never relax for a second.

Most people dread going to a dentist. It isn't so much what

happens as what the patients think will happen that brings on the jitters. Again we have thought-created conditions which we would go a long way to avoid. The *American Weekly*, in its issue of July 7, 1940, told of a Pittsburgh dentist specializing in handling children, who fixed up a children's playroom adjoining his operating room and had it fitted up with toys, sandboxes, blocks, etc. The idea was to get the children interested in playing and thus get their thoughts off the work on their teeth. Once in the chair, the children were encouraged to talk about anything but their teeth. The dentist even attached a button switch to his electric drill line which the children themselves could turn on and off, the dentist assuring them before he started to work that they might turn off the current at the slightest indication of pain. His practice was enormous.

A barber who has built up a large clientele among small children has on his stands numerous children's books, all well-illustrated, which he puts in the hands of his little patrons as he places them in his chair. He gets them interested in the pictures before he starts cutting their hair. "Once in a while it doesn't work," he said, "especially if the child hasn't been taught to look at pictures. Then I have to bring out the mechanical toys, such as those that utter throaty sounds or squeaks when they are squeezed. But the trick is to get the kids to forget about their hair being cut. Once that is done I have no trouble."

Imagination or mental picture-making can often produce queer results. Fear is basically an imaginary factor, as millions of men who went through the war will testify. You suddenly receive a telegram or a long-distance telephone call and before you open the envelope or answer the phone you fear you'll hear bad news—and you promptly get a sinking feeling in the pit of your stomach. The news may be good but for the moment you are shaken with fear and only the good news relieves you of that nervousness.

The story is often told of two men who got the only room left in the hotel. It was ordinarily a storage room, but the hotel, when crowded, used it as a bedroom. During the night one of the men complained of lack of air, and upon arising he groped through the dark to what he thought was the window. He couldn't open it, and, after finding a shoe, knocked out the pane of glass. Then they slept comfortably the rest of the night, only to discover at dawn that the window was intact. What had been smashed was the glass door to a closet!

A somewhat similar story was related during the war by Margaretta West in *This Week Magazine*. She told of returning on a troopship from the South Pacific where she found herself packed into a cabin with seventeen other women. Because of the black-out rules the portholes had been closed, and the cabin was stifling. Inasmuch as the ship was not sailing until morning, permission was granted to open the portholes after everyone was in bed. Miss West tells how she undertook to open the portholes and how everyone was pleased that they could then sleep, and sleep they all did, related Miss West. But, on awakening in the morning, they found that Miss West had opened only the inner porthole, the outer one remaining closed and shutting out both light and air during the night.

During food rationing, thousands of people ate margarine in the home of friends, thinking it to be butter. During prohibition days, it was a common practice to put moonshine whiskey into bottles with labels purporting to be genuine, and many did not know the difference. Sometimes the lowly carp has been served as red snapper, without anyone's being the wiser.

Science has proved in countless ways the effects of the workings of the imagination. Postage stamps have been placed on the skin of patients who believed that they were small mustard plasters; blisters developed under the stamps. By ringing a bell when food was offered to dogs, scientists soon had the animals associating the ringing of the bell with the thought of food, and it was only a short time before it was discovered that the mere ringing of the bell was sufficient to cause their stomachs to secrete digestive juices. Sit at a restaurant counter and notice an enticing dish placed before your neighbor. At once you are hungry and your mouth begins to water.

The peeling of onions often causes tears to flow from the person doing the peeling. Yet the mere sight of an onion being peeled by another person several feet away and with no odor permeating the air will bring tears to the eyes of others in the room. Some people cannot eat warmed-up leftovers, declaring that they make them sick. Undoubtedly, some leftover food that was eaten years before (perhaps it was partly spoiled) did upset their stomachs, and the mental picture never left them. Others claim that they have to take soda after every meal to help digest their food. Medical authorities say that this is often merely the working of their imaginations.

The writer has been across the Atlantic and Pacific Oceans several times and has never been seasick, even in the most severe storms and violent pitchings and rollings of the ship, except once; this was when he had to help another passenger who was violently ill. However, early in his travelings he learned to look away from those who were seasick, realizing that there was a suggestive force that could make him run for the rail. A sudden shock under the pressure of your imagination will cause your skin to turn cold and may even be followed by alternate sweats and chills. Emotional shocks resulting from something your physician has told you have a terrifying effect when your imagination goes to work.

Try whistling sometime when a friend is near you sucking a lemon. The mere sight of it will stop you, and all because the thought of the sour lemon puckers up your mouth and makes whistling impossible.

Often in lecturing, in order to prove the power of the imagination, I would hold up two small bottles, both containing different colored fluids. I would tell my audience that one contained lilac perfume and the other attar of roses, explaining that my experiment was for the purpose of determining the difference in the perceptive powers of my listeners. I would then turn my back on the audience so that they could not see which bottle I was partially emptying into the air; at the same time I called upon them to identify the odor. Some would say lilac, others attar of roses. Of course, there was always great chagrin when both groups discovered that their imaginations had led them astray, and that both bottles contained nothing but colored water, and neither had an odor.

Mark Twain in his little essay, *Concerning Tobacco*, says that a man thinks he can tell what he regards as a good cigar from what he regards as a bad one—but he can't. He goes by the brand, yet imagines he goes by the flavor. Twain, who had the reputation of smoking the worst cigars, tells how he borrowed from a wealthy friend a double handful of forty-cent cigars which bore red-and-gold labels signifying their quality. Twain removed the labels and put the now unbranded cigars into his own box. He passed them out to friends at the end of a dinner and they were all tossed away after two or three whiffs, because his friends believed they were the cheap cigars that Twain smoked. Unquestionably, there is a difference in the taste of even domestic brands of cigars and cigarettes, but the imagination plays an important part in determining it.

When we realize that inventors, artists, scientists, architects, as well as builders of great businesses, employ the imagination, we get some idea of its magnitude. Shakespeare said: "Assume a virtue if you have it not." Now let's take this great truth and follow some of its implications. In assuming a virtue, you are assuming it via your imagination. To become the person you would like to be, you create a mental picture of your newly conceived self, and if you continue to hold it the day will come when you are in reality that person. So it is with the accomplishment of desires.

But here we must make a distinction between daydreaming and a true mental picture, or the proper use of the imagination. Perhaps there is some genie who will drop $100,000 into your lap or overnight provide you with a mansion luxuriously furnished, though the writer has never had the pleasure of meeting one. But daydreaming or mere undirected wishful thinking doesn't have the power to release the latent forces within you that will bring you the one hundred thousand dollars or the mansion. When you employ your imagination properly, you see yourself doing a thing and you go ahead and do it. It's the doing the thing you have pictured to yourself that brings it into actual existence. In this connection, think about the use of a magnifying glass. When properly focused, it will gather the light from the sun and concentrate it, so that the heat will burn a hole in the object upon which the rays are focused. It must be held steady before the heat power is developed. So it is with the holding of the image or the mental picture.

Dr. Emile Coué, the little French doctor who threw so much light on the power of suggestion, declared that imagination was a much stronger force than will-power; when the two are in conflict, he said, the imagination always wins. In explanation, let's say you are an inveterate smoker of good cigars and decide to break yourself of the habit. You grit your teeth, shove out your chin, and solemnly declare that you are going to use your will-power to break yourself of the habit. Then suddenly comes the idea of the taste of a good cigar, its aroma and its soothing effects—the imagination goes to work and the resolution to break the habit goes out the window. The same holds true of efforts to break the drinking habit and other bad habits.

Charles Fourier, a French philosopher of more than a century ago, declared that the future of the world would grow out of the brain of man, shaped, controlled, and directed by the desires and passions by which men are moved. His prophecy is coming true, yet man through his mind has barely started shaping and controlling the world.

All of this brings us to the topic of desire and what you actually want in life. There are comparatively few people with great desires. Most are content to go along filling the tiny niches in which they find themselves. They accept their positions in life as something that fate has fixed for them, and very seldom do they make either a mental or physical effort to extract themselves from those positions. They never raise their sights or realize that it's just as easy to shoot at a bird on a limb thirty feet above the ground as it is to shoot at it on the ground the same distance away. Many engage in wishful thinking, but wishful thinking in itself is without effect simply because the power factor is missing.

But when you run across a person who is "going to town"—and there are many—you realize that the great power behind it all is projected by desire. The way seems easy for those people—and to a great degree it is—because they are putting to use the powers of their subconscious minds which in turn magnetize, co-ordinate, and then transmit to their conscious minds the electrifying vision of the object of their desire.

So let's be reminded that whatever we fix our thoughts upon or steadily focus our imaginations upon, that is what we attract. This is no mere play of words. It is a fact which anyone can prove to his own satisfaction. Whether the results come through magnetic or electrical energy is something still undetermined; while man hasn't been able to define it, manifestations of thought-attraction can be seen on every hand. It is like the electrical field itself—we do not know what electricity is, although in a material sense we know how man can generate it through various kinds of energy-producing apparatus; we see electricity manifest every time we turn on a light or snap a switch.

However, it is very difficult for the average person to concentrate for any length of time, to say nothing of holding on to a mental picture for any great period. You can prove this to yourself in countless ways. You will find that thoughts, ideas, fantasies will ebb and flow through your mind with astonishing rapidity. You are constantly being swayed by what you read, see, and hear, and as a result the co-ordinating part of this creative force turns to gathering together all these scattered elements in a confused mass, instead of devoting itself to making a clear and dynamic picture of your desire.

That brings us to a system of mechanics by which anyone can focus thoughts so that they will penetrate to the deepest depths of the subconscious mind.

The writer has been in the private offices of a great many industrial leaders, business men, great bankers, and others, and long before this science of belief was understood by him, he was impressed with the pictures, photographs, slogans, bits of statuary, and so forth, which were to be found in the inner sanctums of great firms. In the office of the head of a great utility concern are hung the photographs of the early leaders in the industry; in another office are pictures of the great financiers of history; in some there are busts of Napoleon; in others little shrines, good-sized statues of Buddha; and I saw offices where there hung on the walls such slogans as "We do the impossible—any place, any time," "If it can be done, we can do it," "Do it now," "Be a self-starter—don't wait to be cranked." It is reported that F. W. Woolworth, who became known as the Napoleon of business, had his private office in quarters that were a replica of Napoleon's study. Undoubtedly many of you have seen or heard of such displays, but has it ever occurred to you what their purpose was?

There can be only one answer, and that is that they serve as a constant reminder—getting the picture over to the occupant of the room that he too can succeed as did those before him.

He has a motto or a slogan to meet his gaze every time he looks around the room. He sees and feels the eyes of Napoleon upon him when he sits at his desk, or he feels a touch of the spiritual as he gazes at the little shrine. In other words, they are a form of mechanics that the executive uses to excite his imagination, a picture to inspire him, or a series of suggesting forces that reach his subconscious mind. In many a doctor's office (and in some of those who would scoff at the great power of suggestion) hang the photographs of great men of medicine, or famous teachers in medical schools. I have often wondered if the doctors realized the underlying power of these portraits.

When we realize that the subconscious mind is sensitized to the point that it works accurately to externalize the suggestion which is most greatly impressed upon it, we then get a better understanding of the necessity for concentration and for constant repetition of the one suggestion.

In common with other great men, Thomas A. Edison obviously knew the value of the repeated suggestion and made use of it. When his desk, sealed at his death, was opened February 8, 1947, as a part of the ceremonies celebrating the hundredth anniversary of the great inventor's birth, conspicuous among the articles found in it was a piece of paper which bore the legend, "When down in the mouth, remember Jonah, he came out all right." Edison must have thought well of that expression and perhaps reflected much upon it; otherwise he would not have kept it on his desk before him.

Often I have thought of this matter of desire and suggestion in connection with the planting of vegetable or flower seeds. Once the soil is prepared and the tiny seeds are placed in it, it is but a short time when they put forth roots and sprouts begin to appear. The moment they start upward through the soil in search of light, sunshine, and moisture, obstacles mean nothing to them. They will push aside small stones or bits of wood, and if they can't do that, they'll extend themselves and grow around them. They are determined to emerge from the ground. They blossom and give forth fruit, vegetables, or flowers, and they succeed unless some greater force destroys them. While we are not aware of the details of nature's secrets, we observe the seed buried for a long time in the dark gradually expanding and exerting itself until it becomes a thing of beauty or usefulness. Cultivate it, attend it, give it sunshine and water, and it grows into full life. Remember it always produces after its kind, be it single or hybrid.

So with you and the suggestions you impart to your subconscious mind. The result will be pure or complex, depending upon the original seed and the attention which you give it. In other words, plant the right kind of seed—thought of a pure strain—and habitually feed it with strong affirmative thought always directed toward the same end, and it will grow into a mighty force, finding ways and means of overcoming all obstacles. It will reach forth with its roots to find more food on which to grow and expand its foliage to gather more sunshine.

It was desire that brought progress to the world. Without it, we all would still be living in a primitive age. Everything we have in our modern world is the result of desire. Indeed, desire is the motivating force of life itself. You see it all around you—in the animal kingdom, in all forms of plant life, and in all acts and operations of human beings. Hunger promotes a desire for food, poverty a desire for riches, cold causes us to desire warmth, inconveniences a desire for better things.

It's the generating power of all human action, and without it no one can get very far. The keener, the more urgent the desire, the sooner its consummation. It marks the difference between the uneducated ditchdigger and the person of accomplishment, between the clerk and the executive, between the failure and the success. So you must start with desire, keeping in mind that with the magic of believing you can obtain what you picture in your mind's eye. The mechanics are for the purpose of helping you to focus sharply your desire-picture on the screen of your subconscious mind, as well as enable you to shut off and keep out all distracting thoughts, negative ideas, or any fear or doubt projections that might otherwise penetrate to your subconscious.

So let's get down to the mechanics. Secure three or four cards. Ordinary business-size cards will do. In your office, your home, your room, or any other place where you can have privacy, sit down and ask yourself what you desire above everything else. When the answer comes and you are certain that it is your uppermost desire, then at the top of one card write a word picture of it. One or two words may be sufficient—a job, a better job, more money, a home of your own. Then on each card duplicate the word picture on the original. Carry one in your billfold, or handbag, place another alongside your bed or fasten it to your bedstead, place another on your shaving mirror or dressing table, and still another on your desk. The whole idea, as you may have guessed, is to enable you to see mentally the picture at all hours of the day. Just before going to sleep at night and upon waking in the mornings are highly important moments of the twenty-four hours in which to concentrate upon your thoughts with added force. But don't stop with merely those two periods, for the more often you can visualize the desire by this method (or by one of your own devising), the speedier the materialization.

At the start you may have no idea of how the results are to come. Yet you need not concern yourself. Just leave it to the subconscious mind, which has its own ways of making contacts, and of opening doors and avenues that you may never have even thought of. You will receive assistance from the most unexpected sources. You will find that ideas useful in the accomplishment of your program will come at most unexpected times. You may be suddenly struck with the idea of seeing a person you have not heard from for a long time, or calling upon a man you have never seen before. You may get the idea of writing a letter or making a telephone call. Whatever the idea is, follow it. Keep a pad and pencil on a stand near the head of your bed, and when these ideas come during the night, note them on a pad, so they will not be forgotten by morning. Many successful people get ideas during the night that are immediately transcribed to a pad so they will not be lost.

For many years, before I thoroughly understood this science, I was associated with an executive who, after reaching his desk in the morning, would begin pulling notes out of his pocket. In a few minutes things would begin to hum. These notes might contain comments on various advertising media, an outline of a sales campaign, new purchases, or a rearrangement of the sales organization; but all of them contributed to the success of his operations.

If you bear in mind what I told you about successful

executives and their custom of keeping in their offices pictures, mottoes, slogans, busts, and statues, you will appreciate that in using the cards you are utilizing the same forces, only in much more concentrated form.

As I write this, my memory goes back to the time when I put this science to work in order to pull off the rocks the firm of which I was then vice-president. All of the employees sat around in a half-circle, and as I began my remarks I asked each man to provide himself with paper and pencil. Most of them thought that I wanted them to take notes. But there was considerable surprise when I told them to write down what they most wanted in life. I explained that if they would do this, I would point out the way to obtain it. Two or three of the younger men laughed, but the older men, realizing that I was deadly earnest, did as I suggested. To the younger men I said simply: "If you want to hold on to your jobs, you'll do as I ask. For if this stuff doesn't work, we'll all be out on the street." They complied. I told them to show no one what they had written. After the meeting one of the younger men came to me to apologize for having laughed.

"That's all right, Bob," I told him.

"But it sounded so silly at first," he explained. "Imagine me getting a new automobile by simply writing it down. But after you explained the science of it all, I guess it does make sense."

Several years later this chap came to my home and said he wanted to show me something. He did. There along the parking strip was parked his expensive new automobile.

In the years that followed, I found occasion to ask those who attended that meeting if they had obtained what they had written down. Without exception, every man had. One had wanted a wife of a certain nationality. He got her, and there are two fine boys in the family. Another put down the figures of a very sizable fortune. He got it. Another man wanted a beach cottage. Another a better home, and so on. Steadily through the years every one of these men has constantly made money, many of them averaging monthly more than they had ever made before in their lives, much to the astonishment of many others in the same line of business. It cannot be too strongly emphasized that you should tell no one just what the words on the cards mean nor give anyone an inkling of what you desire. To do so may end disastrously for you. When you get a better understanding of this science, you can understand how thought vibrations, consciously or unconsciously, because of envy or some other cause, may be set up to counteract your own.

To illustrate this, I am reminded of a doctor friend who during the early war days applied for a commission in the navy. He closed his office, told everyone that he was joining the navy, and found himself the recipient of many parties and gifts. "It taught me a lesson never to tell anyone of my plans or desires," he laughingly told me later. "It was two years before I received notice of assignment, and during those years I found I had to go back into private practice. It certainly was embarrassing to both myself and family to get various farewell gifts and invitations, only to find that I was to cool my heels at home for two years."

The truth is that when you talk about what you're going to do, you scatter your forces. You lose the close connection with the subconscious, and you frequently find that unless you do as here directed, you will have to start all over again in your program of achievement.

"Go and tell no man" still holds true.

My readers will recall what I said previously about Mumbo Jumbo, chants, incantations, affirmations, etc., and I explained that by engaging in them you put the suggestive forces to work to stimulate your subconscious.

These repetitive words and phrases said silently or aloud are merely methods of convincing the subconscious mind, for autosuggestion, no matter what form, is the only way of molding its pattern. The subconscious is extremely receptive, and it can be convinced of the propositions you present to it, be they true or false, positive or negative; once they are imbedded in the subconscious mind, it goes to work with all of its faculties and energies to materialize them, to make them real in life. The simpler the words to express the ideas you wish conveyed to the subconscious, the better. For example, if you are unhappy, use the words, "I am happy." You don't need the cards for this. Just repeat them to yourself twenty or thirty times. "I am strong," "I am happy," "I am convincing," "I am friendly," "Everything is fine" are a few simple affirmations that you can use to change your mental point of view for the better. But if the effects are to be permanent, the affirmations must be continued until the desired results are obtained.

The person with a fixed goal, a clear picture of his desire, or an ideal always before him, causes it, through repetition, to be buried deeply in his subconscious mind and is thus enabled, thanks to its generative and sustaining power, to realize his goal in a minimum of time and with a minimum of physical effort. Just pursue the thought unceasingly. Step by step you will achieve realization, for all your faculties and powers become directed to that end.

Suppose you want a better job or a promotion. Not only use the cards, but keep telling yourself constantly and continuously that you are going to get that job. You have already visualized it if you have accepted this science, but the repetition will be the means of driving the suggestion deeply and firmly into the subconscious mind. This may be compared to driving a nail into a board. The first tap puts the nail in place, but it is only by a number of heavy strokes that the nail is driven home. Never forget that the subconscious mind will accept and carry out whatever it is powerfully instructed to do. A great example of power developed by repetition is the story of Milo and the calf. Every day he lifted the calf, and then came the day when he was lifting a full-grown bull.

Think of all of this in terms of the so-called material things. You know that two objects cannot fill the same space at the same time. Your mind can be compared to that space: you can't keep your mind filled with negative thoughts or doubts if you have it filled with positive, powerful, and creative thoughts. Consider your mind a room with but a single door and you have the only key. It rests with you to decide who is to come through the door, that is, whether you are dominated by positive or negative thoughts, and which ones you are going to admit, for your subconscious mind will respond to the vibrations of the thoughts that are strongest in you.

Again, compare your mind to a tank filled with clear, unadulterated water. You cannot put any object into that tank without displacing some of the water and causing the tank to overflow. When you permit negative thoughts of doubt or fear to enter your consciousness, it is obvious that the forceful, positive, creative thoughts will have to give way, and consequently you lose your positive state. Thus, so long as you do not permit unfavorable vibrations to reach your subconscious mind, it will not be hindered by anything you may hear, see, or experience. In other words, you must at all times keep your mind filled with positive thoughts so that their strong vibrations will ward off all negative and destructive thoughts that might come from the outside.

For years philosophers have taught that if we are to be happy we must be busy, working or doing something that holds our attention. The explanation lies in the fact that when we are concentrated on some task, our minds are then not open to roving and undesirable vibrations. That is why many doctors advise business and professional men to take up hobbies, in order that their minds may be diverted from worry and trouble thoughts. Others advise trips, new scenes, new personal associations away from the familiar places where it is difficult to get away from disturbing thought vibrations and associations.

As I write, I think of an elderly couple who lost their only son in the Normandy invasion. For months after news of the boy's death was received, the couple kept his room intact just as it was when he left. On Sundays they would spend hours rearranging the furniture and fondly handling his belongings. Was it any wonder, with minds so constantly occupied with the memories of their son, that they became embittered old people? I know what it means to lose loved ones, but I have also learned that it is necessary to close the door on yesterday and keep it closed. We live today, not yesterday.

Now that you have an understanding of how circumstances, environments, and material objectives come into your life through your thinking, it's up to you to make your cherished dreams come true.

Suppose you want a new home. After you've got the first glimpse of the picture, start your affirmations going. Use any expressions you wish, or something like this: "I'm going to have that new home. I'm going to have that new home. I'm going to have that new home." And one day the way will be found and the new home will be yours.

If you're a salesman and want to increase your sales, use the cards, as already suggested, and tell yourself as frequently as possible that you are going to increase your sales. Do it with emphasis.

Strange as it may sound, we usually get what we anticipate, and if we anticipate increasing our sales and believe that we are going to do it, our sales will mount just as though some invisible friend were helping us. The idea of anticipation holds in everything we do.

An insurance man who had increased his business more than 200 per cent within a year after he began using this science, related this story to me: "The sales manager told me to call upon Mr. Blank and not come back to the office until I got an order out of him. This prospect was a hard nut to crack, as everyone knew. He had the reputation of being a very stubborn and cranky individual with little time for salesmen, to say nothing of us in the insurance business. However, I knew that he had lots of property and had to carry all sorts of fire and liability coverage. As I went down the stairs from our office and all the way up the street to this prospect's office, I kept repeating to myself: 'Fred, you're going to sell him, you're going to sell him. You're going to find him a fine old fellow, no matter what anyone says. He's going to be friendly and he's going to accept what you have to offer.' Maybe I repeated those ideas a couple of hundred times. Not only did he turn out to be very cordial, but I came away with an order for a $25,000 policy, the first our company had ever secured from the old man."

This insurance man has long since left the agency with which he was connected and now has a firm of his own, with a country estate he is rapidly developing into a showplace. A short time ago he told me that he was "fixed financially for life."

Dale Carnegie has told of the great success of Howard Thurston, the magician. According to the story, in going out on the stage Thurston would repeatedly say to himself that he loved his audience and that he was going to give them the best that was in him. He made two million dollars!

Another man—he's seventy-eight but doesn't look more than sixty—who is a profound student of this subject, and who used it to make a tremendous fortune for himself, but whose interests today are along other lines, declares that he still orders his subconscious mind to "get busy for him."

"I talk to it just as I might be talking to some individual to whom I was giving orders. And I never have any doubts or fears that it will not do as ordered. If I get an upset stomach, I simply tell it to be itself and act naturally; so with other ailments that arise. If I want to awaken at five o'clock in the morning without using an alarm clock, I peremptorily order my subconscious mind to awaken me. It has never failed in anything so far.

"I have long had a theory that the subconscious mind controls our age—what I mean is that for centuries the subconscious mind has been led to believe that a man should be old when he is sixty. For most people who have accepted the thought, it can't be otherwise, for that is what the subconscious mind believes. However, in my case I refuse to accept it and, as you know, I am as active as I was when I was fifty years old—and I expect to carry on for some years to come."

All of which shows the advisability of not implanting in your subconscious mind the idea that you are becoming old and incapable merely because the years are passing; it also shows that by keeping the subconscious free from the fixed idea of a decline, you improve your chances of prolonging your life far beyond the so-called allotted span.

Repetition is the fundamental rhythm of all progress, the cadence of the universe. It's the chuff-chuff of the locomotive that takes a train across the continent, it's the repeated explosions that generate power in the automobile engine, the airplane, the rocket gun, the robot bomb. It's the constant surging of the water against the turbine blades that generates electrical power. It's the tap-tap of the hammer that drives the nail into place. It's the deadly put-put of the machine gun that mows down everything before it. It's the constant and determined effort that breaks down all resistance, sweeps away all obstacles. It's the repeated auto- or heterosuggestion that makes you and others believe. It's the tap-tap of the same conscious thought that causes it to be impressed upon your subconscious mind and on the subconscious minds of others.

While anyone can demonstrate the efficacy of the repeated suggestion, whether it be used either constructively or destructively, the words of Professor Hugo Münsterberg, Harvard psychologist, throw considerable light on its value. He said:

"The value of repetition must distinctly be understood in the relation of the inner-setting and the inner mental attitude."

Before World War II there was in Paris a famous institute devoted to the teaching of suggestion by means of phonograph records. They were played over and over again, and the listeners could hear any record they wanted—records that gave them the repeated suggestion that they were in good health, that they had the power to overcome their difficulties, that they could receive help in other ways.

For years mothers have been taught to talk to their babies and small children while they were asleep, repeating such suggestions as that they were going to grow well and strong, that they were to develop certain good habits, that they were to become good citizens. In view of the fact that the children were asleep, obviously the suggestions were directed to their subconscious minds.

In the destruction of Carthage, the greatest maritime power of the ancient world, we have an instance of the power of the repeated suggestion at work. Cato, the great Roman statesman, convinced that Rome and Carthage could not both survive, ended every speech in the Senate with the words, "Carthage must be destroyed!" He kept it up until the Romans were saying in their sleep, "Carthage must be destroyed"—and Carthage was destroyed.

Many people become confused and frustrated because they allow themselves to be influenced by negative thoughts of others—this is a weakness of many salesmen—when they absorb too much of what the prospect says about his reasons for not doing something such as buying. Repetition of negative thoughts will discourage even the most powerful if continued long enough, and unless your mind is closed against them and you counteract them by constantly thinking and radiating positive thoughts, you will sooner or later find yourself sunk. Some people wear themselves out trying to combat these negative forces by superhuman effort and sheer will-power, never realizing that their own minds, operating in accordance with the suggestive influences, are causing all the trouble.

Whether we know it or not, we are all victims of suggestion, in many cases almost to the point of being hypnotized. We follow along a beaten path of living just because we've been doing it for decades. We wear certain styles of clothing, hold to certain customs, all because we have been led to believe, through the never-ending suggestive thoughts that come to us from all sides, that that is the thing to do. Houses, churches, office buildings, automobiles, buses, streetcars for years followed a certain pattern, and yet, when someone gets off the beaten path with a new way of doing things, he is considered a crank or an eccentric. What I refer to, on close analysis, as mass hypnosis is seen around us in every human activity.

It has been my observation that those who consciously use this science (as well as those who may be using it unconsciously) are people of tremendous energies, virtually human dynamos. There are people who not only use their imaginations and hold strong beliefs and convictions, but they are great doers in action. And that brings me to this most important statement: "Faith without action is dead."

Unquestionably, there are people on this earth who by concentrated thought and by thought alone—without moving from their offices or making any contacts, personal or otherwise, with other people—can achieve remarkable things. But in the main, this so-called material world of ours is controlled by men of action—great dynamos of energy that energize others. Nicola Tesla, who probably understood the laws of vibration better than any other man of his time, declared that he could, with a machine that could be slipped into his pocket, cause the Empire State Building in New York to disintegrate and fall apart. (As a matter of fact, the operation of a somewhat similar bit of apparatus did cause buildings to shake, windows to break, furniture to move, in lower New York when Tesla was first experimenting with it during the eighteen-nineties.) That machine came out of Mr. Tesla's mind. His thoughts created it. Here is an example of a man who coupled his "faith with action."

There are metaphysicians and teachers of the occult who claim that a person can sit in his own office and visualize orders pouring on to his desk—and the orders will quickly materialize; but to accomplish it, the mental picture or thought projection must be definite and unwavering, and *that* requires great practice and concentration. Stranger things have been recorded. But for the person who has not yet developed this mind-power, it is well to add action and energy to his efforts by doing the things, following out the ideas, and by making the contacts which are dictated by his subconscious mind.

Many years ago I read that Franklin D. Roosevelt constantly made use of his subconscious mind, and I am certain that he knew much about the use of the repeated suggestion. He never looked "backward," but always "forward"— "yesterday" was a closed book. On April 17, 1945, Kirke L. Simpson, an Associated Press Staff Writer and an intimate of the late President, told of a party given Roosevelt after he had been stricken with infantile paralysis. Mr. Simpson said that Mr. Roosevelt was determined to walk again, somehow, anyhow, without crutches. His intimates, according to Mr. Simpson, decided to give him a cane as a token that they, too, expected him to walk again, and after it was presented the President sat all evening with the cane cuddled against his shoulder. Mr. Simpson said that he would reach up to pat its crook now and then, and "we knew that he was saying to himself: 'You'll walk again, Frank Roosevelt; you will walk again!' "

Roosevelt firmly believed in the power of believing, as is apparent in an article in *Time* magazine (March 4, 1946). It told of a letter written by him in 1924 to a doctor seeking advice on the treatment of infantile paralysis. Mr. Roosevelt pointed out that he thought gentle exercise, massage, and sun-bathing were essential. "But," he added, "more important than most therapy is a 'belief on the patient's part that he will eventually recover.' " Here we have a wonderful example of the magic of believing at work, and, as I have pointed out, of the part the "repeated suggestion" plays in establishing belief.

CHAPTER VI

The Mirror Technique for Releasing the Subconscious

THE TOUGHEST PROBLEM that confronts most people is the lack of money, and while I have read and heard of people finding bundles of $1000 bills by using this Mind Stuff, I think that money comes as a result of combining Mind Stuff and energized action. Money certainly can be attracted by your thought, and once it appears on the horizon your thought will lead you to ways and means of acquiring it. While I was in the investment banking business I knew many people of large means, and I found that every one of them had a "money consciousness." They *thought* wealth and their coming to possess it was quite similar to my own experience related earlier in this book.

It is always the same technique, no matter what your desires. Get the picture of what you want and keep telling yourself that you're going to get it. But don't think it is going to come to you if you merely indulge in a period of watchful waiting. Go to work, always keeping your goal in mind, and start saving. Every dollar you save out of your weekly pay check is a step nearer to the fortune that is going to be yours. Consider it as such and save as many dollars as you can. The more you save, the faster you will build that fortune. Then put your savings out at interest, invest them where they will work advantageously for you, not by gambling or playing the market, but in securities of proven worth, in real estate, or in a business of your own. As your investment grows under your money consciousness, you'll be agreeably surprised to find that the more you have, the more you accumulate. Furthermore, you'll find it exciting and stimulating. Opportunities for profitable investments will come to you from many unexpected and unknown sources, but don't make the mistake that many do and follow will-o'-the-wisps; get sound advice before you invest a cent.

I recall one woman and her daughter who in twenty-five years accumulated more than half a million dollars, which today is largely represented by apartment houses and store buildings. The woman's husband died shortly after World War I, and she was left with a fairly large-sized house. She was at her wits' end how to support herself and her daughter who had just finished high school. She had no previous experience in holding a job or carrying on a business, but she could cook and keep house. One morning the idea came to her to take in roomers and boarders. That was the start, and success came rapidly. Within two years she sold the house and the business, realizing a handsome profit, and then bought a much larger house directly across the street from a well-known men's club, believing that with her high-grade cooking she could get much of the club's overflow business. She did—and prospered; even though she employed plenty of help, no task was too lowly for her in a rush period.

A retired elderly business man who had taken up his home at her place one day suggested that she open a tea room. He said he would provide the necessary funds to fix up a place. The top floor of an office building in the business section was found and the tea room opened. With herself as hostess and her daughter as cashier during the rush hours, and at other times helping in the kitchen and directing her employees, she soon made the tea room a favorite eating-place for business men. That led to the purchase of a beach hotel through a mortgage company, and also to the profitable sale of the tea room. All of this time she was investing in securities and it wasn't long before she had accumulated a nest egg of $25,-000, which went as the first payment on a run-down apartment house. Remodeling under her direction made the building remarkably attractive, and it became very popular under her management. With the great results achieved her reputation came to the attention of an insurance company that owned other apartment houses in those days, and she was offered the management of a number of them on a salary and a percentage basis. As her capital grew, her opportunities to buy apartment houses followed, and the last time I heard of this woman with the "money-consciousness" she not only owned apartment houses in this particular city, but she had also purchased an apartment house at a near-by beach resort which previously had operated only during the summer months, but which she now operates all the year round.

It has long been my observation that a person with a workable idea seldom has any difficulty in getting money to finance himself. However, he must be thoroughly "sold" on the idea himself before he can convince others to lend him money. If you contemplate having your own business, think about this and use the science of belief, for you'll find someone with money who will help you.

Great fortunes are not built in a day but come as a result of dollars adding themselves to those you already have or to those you earn and save. But if you want a fortune, you must put your mind and energies to work. It will come—just use the magic of believing.

Here's another case where by using this science success followed in rapid order—in fewer than ten years. A corner druggist had gone into bankruptcy. The fixtures were owned by the owner of the building and most of the stock by a wholesale druggist. A young pharmacist heard about the location, but had no funds with which to proceed. Finally the wholesaler and the landlord got together, and the young fellow "sold himself" to both of them. The landlord, anxious to keep the place occupied, agreed to finance the young fellow for several months, and with necessary guarantees to the wholesaler the place was reopened. His wife helped behind the counter and at the fountain and the business began to grow. For a long time the young druggist had been interested in a preparation which he thought would help people, but he had never had the funds to finance himself. One day he decided to talk with the owner of the building, a man of considerable wealth. So thoroughly did he believe in his plan that he had no trouble in convincing the owner, who organized a company for the young fellow and put up $5000 to start. For months the preparation was bottled in the basement of the rented home of the druggist during evenings after the store was closed. People began to buy it in increasing quantities and the business began to expand. It spread all over the country, and within a few years not only was the landlord paid off, but he told me that his profit was better than $50,000 and that the young fellow's income was now more that $100,000 a year. He and his company now own the building where he started.

Another remarkable story came to my attention a few years back in the midst of the so-called depression. The story is from the man's own lips. He had been in clerical positions most of his life but one day found himself on the WPA payroll. His wife in an endeavor to get help for some of her troubles had taken up "religion." The religious organization was one that insists upon tithing—that is, upon the payment by each member of 10 per cent of his income.

(By the way, there are thousands of people who are firm believers on tithing, and, as a matter of fact, one of our greatest industrialists, who preaches religion in his own organization and to outsiders, attributes much of his success to his practice of tithing. Another man who is very successful in the selling of baking machines and equipment, credits his success entirely to his tithing. Whether this giving of one-tenth of their income to the church or to some religious or charitable organization has anything to do with the success of these individuals, is, of course, something that the writer cannot answer; but surely these tithers believe thoroughly in the efficacy of their practices, and who is there to say that it doesn't work for them?)

One night the husband on WPA was prevailed upon to accompany his wife to church and then "the light hit me," as he told me. Upon arriving at his home, "something" led him to search for an old formula which his father had used in preparing a lotion or a tonic that could be used in all barber and beauty shops. With the finding of the formula, he began to gather old bottles from junk-shops and scrap piles, which he took home and washed—and they became the first containers. This man went personally from barbershop to barbershop, from beauty parlor to beauty parlor, and so convincing were his stories that it wasn't long before he gave up his WPA job and opened up a plant of his own. He believed thoroughly that the tithing principle was responsible for his good fortune and for all of the ideas that came to him. His product became widely known throughout the country, but the trade was no longer supplied by the man personally— wholesalers pushed it and he had his own sales organization as well. Another illustration of the magic of believing.

Everything on the material plane is first an idea, a thought in someone's mind. A person selling a commodity is actually selling an idea—if it's a machine, what the machine will do—if building material, how it can be used—if food, how nutritious and tasty it will be, and so on endlessly. All businesses, all fortunes are the outgrowth of an idea, the workings of someone's imagination followed by action.

For years I have watched the progress of the Jantzen Knitting Mills, makers of the famous Jantzen swimming suits. I have seen this manufacturing concern grow from practically nothing but an idea to an organization that circles the globe, and the success story of those behind it rivals any told by Horatio Alger. Several times I've discussed this science with J. A. Zehntbauer, president of the company and chairman of its board, and with his permission I quote a letter he wrote to me:

As you say, some people seem to possess an indefinable something which spurs them on to a successful and happy life, while others apparently work hard but without that something in their characters which brings them satisfaction and success.

I have never tried systematically to develop this indefinable spirit but believe it has been developed in me by my parents, and especially by my mother, who promptly fought our inclination as youngsters to say, "I can't do this or I can't do that," by saying to us that we should not say we can't do it, but that, of course, we can do anything anyone else can do, and all that was necessary was to tackle the job and keep on trying until it was mastered; and that we would then be ready to tackle a bigger job, and to shrink from no job because it was great or unimportant. Then she was constantly resisting our inclination as youngsters to complain or growl about anything. When we were in a complaining disposition, she would say, "Don't grumble but think what a privilege it is to live in such a wonderful world and instead of complaining, brace right up and keep smiling and enjoy the blessings at hand."

There were four youngsters in our family, three boys and one girl. We have always been exceptionally happy and I attribute it to the training of our parents; mother, with her constant training and father corroborating her often by saying: "Always look on the bright side, never on the dark side of things."

If one has not been fortunate enough to have the advantages of such influences, I can see where it would take a great amount of self-discipline and training to bring one up to the point of view which you clearly point out is necessary to get the most out of life. Regardless of one's present circumstances, I am sure the application of your science would be valuable to him.

In a postwar world, the competition is unusually keen and naturally the person best prepared for a certain position is in a far better position to get it than one who is not. I say this because I do not wish to give the idea to any of my readers that a man who has had neither the education nor the experience can step out of the army, or out of a job in an industrial plant, and immediately take over the reins of a large industrial corporation simply by using this science of belief. There may be exceptional cases of men doing this, but they are few and far between.

First things come first, always, and if a man feels and believes he is entitled to a better job and has prepared himself for it, then with the use of this science he can get that job or some other as good or better.

A well-known executive once said to me, "The difficulty I see with most people seeking employment is that they are so wrapped up in themselves that they make no effort to impress their prospective employer with what they can do to help him, overlooking the fact that the other fellow is only interested in you to the extent that you can help him."

To some of my readers this may appear a cold-blooded attitude, but in the world of competition, self-interest is a reality that all prospective employees must face.

There is an old saying that "If you do not follow your own thoughts, then you will follow the thoughts of the fellow who followed his," and it means exactly what it says—it marks the difference between a leader and a follower. You who do not think or use your creative ability are always being given orders by those who do. Unless you are willing to think, you will have to labor physically, and this means you will receive less for your work.

Therefore, visualize the kind of job you want, and use your cards and your constant affirmations until belief in your goal becomes a vital part of you and you feel it in your blood, your bones, and in every tissue of your body. See yourself actually doing the things you visualize and it will all work out, because every thought held constantly and persistently sooner or later materializes after its kind. All of you sometime in your life have taken vacation trips. Did you ever stop to analyze the mental processes involved? First you got the idea of the trip, then you decided where you would go, and shortly you began to visualize yourself in the mountains, at the seashore, or visiting some new city, and the vacation turned out as planned because you saw yourself doing it—actually before the vacation trip became a reality. Could anything be clearer? Whatever you want to do, just apply the same principles and you will get the same successful results.

You will remember the card device, which I explained in detail. There is another device, which I call the mirror technique. Before explaining it, I want to tell you how I happened to discover what a truly wonderful thing it is, and how it can be used to bring quicker and more effective results.

Many years ago I was the dinner guest of a very wealthy man who owned many patents covering logging and sawmill machinery. He had invited a number of newspaper publishers, bankers, and industrial leaders to his suite in a prominent hotel, in order to explain a new method he had devised for mill operations. Liquor flowed freely and it wasn't long before the host himself was very much intoxicated. Just before dinner was served, I noticed him staggering into his bedroom and pulling himself up abruptly before his dresser. Thinking that I might help him, I followed him to the door of his room. As I stood there, I saw him grab the edge of the dresser top with both hands and stare into the mirror, all the time mumbling as a drunken man sometimes does. Then his words began to make sense and I moved back a little to watch the performance. I heard him say: "John, you old———, they tried to get you drunk, but you're going to fool them. You're sober, you're sober, cold sober, this is your party and you've got to be sober."

As he kept repeating these words, while continuing to stare at the reflection of his eyes in the mirror. I noticed that a transfiguration was taking place. His body was becoming more erect, the muscles of his face were tightening, and his drunken look was disappearing. The whole performance was over in perhaps five minutes, but in all my experience as a newspaper man and more especially as a police reporter where I had opportunity to observe many drunken people, I had never seen such a rapid change. Not wanting him to know that I had observed him, I made for the bathroom. When I got back to the dining room I found the host at the head of the table, and while his face was still a little flushed, to all appearances he was sober. At the end of the dinner he presented a very dramatic and convincing picture of his new plans. It wasn't until long afterward, when I got a better understanding of the power of the subconscious mind, that I understood the science involved in transforming the obviously drunken man into a cold-sober host.

I have for many years given the mirror technique to thousands of people, with some very unusual results. During these years a large number of people came to me for help with their problems. There were a surprising number of women, and practically all of them started their stories with weeping spells. The first thing I did was to stand them before a full-length mirror and have them take a good look at themselves; I made them look into their eyes and tell me what they saw there—crybabies or fighters? Their crying soon ceased, and those cases convinced me that a woman cannot weep while looking at herself in a mirror. Whether it be pride, shame, or the repudiated idea that they are weaklings that stops them short, is of no moment. The fact remains that the tears cease flowing.

Many great orators, preachers, actors, and statesmen have used this mirror technique for years. Winston Churchill, according to Drew Pearson, never made a speech of importance unless he made it before a mirror first. Pearson also declared that Woodrow Wilson employed the same technique. It's what I call a supercharging method of stepping up the subconscious forces of the speaker so that when he appears before an audience those forces flow out to and affect his listeners. By using the mirror in rehearsing the speech as you are going to deliver it, you are creating at that moment a picture of yourself, your words, the sound of your voice, and your sight of the audience, to which the immediate future is to bring reality. By looking into the mirror, you increase the mental vibrations by which the force and meaning of your words will quickly penetrate to the subconscious minds of your audience.

This mirror technique gives a clue to the power and the personal magnetism of Billy Sunday, the evangelist. I knew Bill Sunday in his heyday and often heard him preach, but in those days, knowing little or nothing about this Mind Stuff, I was puzzled as to how he, as well as Gypsy Smith and other great evangelists, was able to influence people to such a remarkable degree.

However, we now have proof that Billy Sunday was versed in the use of the mirror technique; it is given by Eric Sevareid, Columbia Broadcasting System commentator, in his book *Not So Wild a Dream*, published in 1946. Mr. Sevareid tells how he as a young newspaper reporter secured an interview with Billy Sunday.

"He bounded about the hotel room, now peering intently out of the window, with one foot on the sill, now grasping the dressing-table firmly in both hands while *lecturing his reflection in the mirror.*"

One of the most outstanding insurance salesmen in America who early accepted the science of belief told me that he never called upon an important prospect without first giving his sales presentation in front of a mirror. His sales were phenomenal.

Every salesman has heard the statement, "If you can convince yourself, you can convince the other fellow," which is basically true. Every great mass movement in history from religious to military has come about through one individual, whose flaming belief in his own cause gave him the power to convert thousands of others. A man need not be a student of psychology to know that enthusiasm is very contagious and can readily be transmitted to others if one is bursting with it. The mirror technique is a simple and effective method by which a person can strengthen his belief in his own sales ability and thus intensify the power of his enthusiasm.

When the mirror technique is considered in the light of the science given in this book, it becomes a master method by which the mighty forces of the subconscious mind can be employed to influence those with whom you are dealing.

Whether we know it or not, we're all engaged in selling something—if not our wares, then our personalities, our services, our ideas. As a matter of fact, all human relationships are based upon selling of one kind or another, and we all engage in it whenever we undertake to persuade others to our way of thinking. Legally a contract or an agreement is based upon a "meeting of the minds," and unless you can get the other person to think your way, you do not get very far. But once the minds meet on the major issues, the rest is easy, and the name on the dotted line is but a matter of a few more moments.

During the "depression" days when I was working with many business and sales organizations to increase their business, I introduced this mirror method with some startling results. In one concern, a pie-making organization, I had mirrors fastened to the inside of the back doors of all the trucks, so that when the driver-salesmen opened the doors to get their goods for delivery, the first thing to be seen was the mirrors. I always admonished each man to determine before calling upon a customer how many pies he was going to sell him, and then to tell himself in the mirror that pies to that number would be left on the customers' counters. One driver told me that for many months he had been trying to sell one woman restaurant owner, but she had always refused to purchase. Then he decided to try the mirror technique. That day he sold her ten pies. At the time he related his story to me he was selling her an average of fifteen pies daily.

The mirror technique was used with great effectiveness in insurance companies, financial houses, rubber mills, automobile agencies, cookie manufacturing plants, and many other organizations where there were salesmen or where there was a combination of salesmen and production operators. In my own old organization, where a complete about-face movement had to be made to avert disaster, I first used this technique by placing a mirror in a back room of the office where the employees left their hats and overcoats. It was so placed that everyone had to see it when entering or leaving the room. At first I pasted strips of paper with such slogans as "We're going to win," "Nothing is impossible to an indefatigable mind," "We've got the guts, let's prove it," "Let's show the world we're not licked and then go to town," How many are you going to sell today?" and a great many others. We then took to using soap to write the slogans directly on the face of the mirror. Every morning a new slogan appeared, with the sole purpose of convincing our employees that they could get business even though other firms in the same line were having a struggle to keep their doors open. Later this setup was augmented by a second mirror placed alongside the doorframe of the main door to the office, which would always be the last thing seen by the salesmen as they left the office. Subsequently I had mirrors placed alongside calendar frames on the desks of all salesmen and executives, and the startling thing about it all was that during the worst of the "depression" days the salesmen—and I mean all of them—trebled and quadrupled their incomes, and they have maintained their progress ever since. There are a number of men whose monthly income probably never exceeded in the best of times $300 who now and for several years have averaged better than $1000 a month. This may sound incredible to some of my readers, but it's true. In my files are many letters from executives, salesmen, and others who have testified to the effectiveness of the mirror idea.

Now to outline the technique. Stand in front of a mirror. It need not be a full-length mirror, but it should be of sufficient size so that you may at least see your body from the waist up.

Those of you who have been in the army know what it means to come to attention—stand fully erect, bring your heels together, pull in your stomach, keep your chest out and your head up. Now breathe deeply three or four times until you feel a sense of power, strength, and determination. Next, look into the very depths of your eyes, tell yourself that you are going to get what you want—name it aloud so you can see your lips move and you can hear the words uttered. Make a regular ritual of it, practice doing it at least twice a day, mornings and evenings—and you will be surprised at the results. You can augment this by writing with soap on the face of the mirror any slogans or key words you wish, so long as they are the key to what you have previously visualized and want to see in reality. Within a few days you will have developed a sense of confidence that you never realized you could build within yourself.

If you are planning to call on an exceptionally tough prospect or are proposing to interview the boss whom you may have previously feared, use the mirror technique, and keep it up until you are convinced that you can make the proper presentation without any trepidation. And of course, if you are called upon to make a speech, by all means practice before a mirror. Gesticulate—pound your fist on the palm of your other hand to drive home the arguments—use any other gestures that come naturally to you.

As you stand before the mirror, keep telling yourself that you are going to be an outstanding success and that nothing in this world is going to stop you. Does this sound silly? Don't forget that every idea presented to the subconscious mind is going to be produced in its exact counterpart in objective life, and the quicker your subconscious gets the idea, the sooner your wish becomes a picture of power. Certainly it is not good business for you to tell anyone of the devices you employ, because you might be ridiculed by scoffers and your confidence shaken, especially if you are just beginning to learn the science.

If you are an executive or sales manager and you want to put more push into your entire organization, teach your employees the mirror technique and see that they use it, just as many organizations now do.

Much has been written about the power of the eyes. The eyes are said to be the windows of the soul; they reveal your thoughts. They express you far more than you imagine. They permit others to "get your number," as the saying goes. However, you will find that once you start this mirror practice your eyes will take on a power that you never realized you could develop (something that writers have referred to as a dynamic or fascinating power); this power will give you that penetrating gaze that causes others to think you are looking into their very souls. Sooner or later there will come an intensity that will bespeak the intensity of your thought, which people will begin to recognize. It will be recalled that Emerson wrote that every man carries in his eye the exact indication of his rank. Remember that your own gradation or position in life is marked by what you carry in your eyes. So develop eyes that bespeak confidence. The mirror will help you.

This mirror technique may be used in many different ways and with very gratifying results. If you have a poor posture, or are slovenly in your talk, you will find that practice before a full-length mirror will work wonders for you. Your mirror shows you the person others see when they look at you, and you can fashion yourself into any kind of person you would like them to see.

It is said that if you act the part you will become that part, and here again there is no better way than rehearsing your acting before the mirror. Vanity has no part in this science. Consequently, don't use the mirror in a supercilious manner, but use it to build yourself into the person you wish to be. Surely, if some of the world's most outstanding men and women use this mirror technique to build themselves and increase their influence over other people, you can use it for your own special requirements.

Much has been written about intuition, hunches, and the like. Some psychologists claim that ideas which come to us intuitively are not something "out of the blue," but come as a result of our accumulated knowledge or because of something we may have seen or heard in earlier times. That may be true to some extent with chemists, inventors, and others who work by the "trial and error" method of using their knowledge and the results of previous experiments, but it's the writer's belief that by far the greatest number of discoveries, illuminations, and inspired works come from the subconscious mind, without previous knowledge having been planted in the mind. Every custom we follow, everything we utilize was first an idea in someone's mind, and those ideas came first in the way of "hunches," intuitive flashes, or call them what you will. So it is wise to heed your intuitions and to trust them to the end.

Many great leaders, industrialists, and inventors have openly declared that they have followed the hunches which have come to them in odd moments of relaxation or in periods when they were engaged in some other task than trying to solve their problems. A good way to let your subconscious mind solve a problem is for you to tackle it from all angles consciously; then some night just before dropping off to sleep, order the subconscious mind to bring you the answer. You may awaken in the middle of the night with the answer, or it may come to you upon awakening in the morning or at some odd moment of the day when you are engaged in something quite different. Be quick to grasp it when it comes and waste no time in following through with it.

You may have a hunch to call on or telephone a certain man. He may be the head of some concern and in a position to be of great help to you. However, because of his position you may fear to make the move and you struggle with your "hunch" on one hand and your fear on the other. The fear too often wins. The next time fear or doubt enters your mind, ask yourself this question: "What have I got to lose if I do see him or call him? What harm can I do?" Your fears and doubts can't answer that question. So obey your hunch without delay.

A word of warning should be given here, however. Many people like to gamble. Some play cards, others bet on the horse or dog races, and many play the market. Undoubtedly there are those who say that they follow their hunches and now and then make a "killing," but the writer urges you not to use your hunches in an endeavor to get something for nothing. There is something fundamentally wrong about it, because most gamblers die broke. Also, beware of hunches that would lead you into untried fields. They may not be hunches at all, but just sudden fanciful longings. The true kind of hunch is always concerned with something that is related to you directly or indirectly, and it gives you the idea to do a certain thing, followed by the momentum to carry out the necessary action.

The writer takes it for granted that none of his readers will assume that this book is an open-sesame to riches and fame overnight. It is intended only as a key to unlock the door that opens on the roadway which will lead to the goal of your desire. Certainly it wouldn't be wise to rush into undertakings far beyond your capabilities or your development. If you would be the head of a great utility concern, you would naturally have to know the business, just as you would if you aspired to become head of a huge transportation system. But by using this science, you could learn the various steps which would take you to the top. However, you must have a plan of action before any program is undertaken. You wouldn't go to the corner drugstore and ask just for drugs. You would be specific and name the drugs desired. And so it is with this science. You must have a plan of action—you've got to know what you want and be specific about it.

If you have definitely determined what you want and have fixed a goal for yourself, then consider yourself extremely fortunate, for you have taken the first step that will lead to success. As long as you hold on to the mental picture of your idea and begin to develop it with action, nothing can stop you from succeeding, for the subconscious mind never fails to obey any order given to it clearly and emphatically.

CHAPTER VII

How to Project Your Thoughts

SUCCESS IS a matter of never-ceasing application. You must forever work at it diligently. Otherwise it takes wings and flies away. At no time can you afford to rest on your laurels—a pause for self-admiration—because there are others who may have eyes on your coveted place and who would like nothing better than to push you out of it, especially if they observe that you have a weak hold on it or are doing nothing to strengthen your position.

Despite the great strides that America has made, it is still a country with great resources, many of which have not yet been tapped. Even though the war, with its atomic bombs, radar, rocket guns and ships, amphibious boats, and daring uses of plastics and metals opened up a mighty unexplored field where still greater things will be accomplished by men with imaginations and the spirit-to-do, the writer believes that "we haven't seen anything yet"; those of us who are alive fifty years hence will be looking upon a world which in comparison will make the early postwar years look like the Stone Age.

Already in our laboratories scientists are at work on what many may consider fantastic ideas. These include light and wearable fabrics from wood and other products that will be fire- and water-resistant, materials that will make ships unsinkable, machines that will capture energy from the sun, and even apparatus that will actually record our unspoken thoughts. These are only a few of the things appearing on the horizon, and they are all coming from the imaginations of men, or from their subconscious minds. Perhaps in less than fifty years thought-transference or telepathy will be as commonplace as the radio of today. Who knows?

It has been said that man can bring into materialization anything that he can conceive mentally, and the millions of things we use and enjoy today prove it. When man fully comprehends the great power of his mind and earnestly puts it to work, not only will he have dominion over this earth and everything on it, but he may be reaching out to control the near-by planets. You yourself have this inner spark, but it must be fanned until the fire is of white-heat intensity and it must be constantly stoked, which you do by adding fuel— ideas, ideas, more ideas, and action.

One man I know who has many achievements to his credit and who has passed the seventy mark, declared that most people fall by the wayside because they are never starting anything. "I make it a plan, and have for years, to start something new—that is, new for me—at least once a week. It may be only the making of some simple gadget for use in the kitchen or it may be an entirely new sales plan or reading an unfamiliar book. I find in following this plan not only that I keep my body and mind active, but also that I put to use a lot of imaginative qualities that otherwise might fall asleep and atrophy. This idea of a man's retiring when he's sixty is to me a great mistake. As soon as a man retires and quits being active mentally and physically, he's on the way to his grave in short order. You have seen what has happened to fire horses when they are retired. You know what happens to your automobile when you leave it outside unused and neglected; it starts to rust and is soon headed for the junkshop. Humans are the same; they rust out or wither and die when they go on the shelf."

The plan of starting something new at least once a week brings us to the matter of initiative and how valuable an asset individual initiative is for any person who seeks success. Without it a man is stopped almost as soon as he starts. Men and women remain in minor clerical positions all of their lives because they never display initiative in their work, never attempt to find new ways of doing their work, and never suggest improvements. During the war a number of organizations placed suggestion boxes in their plants and offered prizes for those suggestions that were considered most practical. Frequently these suggestions led to greatly improved methods in plant operations, as well as rewards in advancement for the employees offering the suggestions. In a number of instances employee suggestions led to patentable devices that brought fame and fortune to those supplying the initial ideas. Bear in mind that no matter how long a piece of work has been done in a certain way, there's always a better way. The war demonstrated that, so give heed to initiative. Even if you are just a clerk behind the counter in some store, you certainly must have some ideas of how goods may be better displayed or how the customers may be better served. Good ideas for lighting, color schemes, arrangement of the counters, display shelves are always acceptable to management, and are rewarded.

Closely linked with this matter of initiative are interest and attention. The more interest you take in your work, naturally the more attention you give it and the greater are the results. We all know that we do best the things in which we are interested, so if you do not find the task before you of interest, look for one that will interest you. The more absorbing the interest, the better—the interest factor alone will give you momentum that will carry you a long way forward.

One woman I know who was employed in a large department store as assistant to the manager of one of its largest departments, although her salary was fixed under the wartime ceiling, for several years received the store's highest Christmas bonus because of her interest and initiative, and her advice, rather than that of the manager of the department, was often sought by the head of the store.

The personnel manager of a huge defense plant employing many thousands of both men and women told me that the greatest fault he had to find with people was that they could not be depended upon. Some fail to keep their word, others are always late for their engagements, still others are forever changing their minds. So if you tell another person that you are going to do a certain thing, even though its fulfillment may cause you some inconvenience, do it no matter what the consequences or the cost in time or energy. You will be amply repaid, for you are building a reputation for reliability, which will be of great value as you proceed up the ladder.

Many employees hold to the idea that their work is given to them merely that they may further the interests of their employers. They never entertain the thought that they are actually working for themselves, the employer merely furnishing the tools and the place for the employee to work. There is an old saying that unless a man has learned to take orders he can never learn to give them. How true this is; but how few, working day after day, ever realize that it is within their own power to sit some day in the executive's place and give orders.

"The only way to have a friend is to be one," said Emerson; but few people ever give thought to this fundamental requirement. You can't cast your bread upon the waters without having it returned, and you can't do a good deed without having a good deed done to you in return; this is true, no matter how Pollyanna-ish it may sound to some people.

Rare indeed is the man who doesn't make an enemy now and then. You get out of tune with a man or perhaps he gets out of tune with you. Naturally, you don't like him; as a result of your thinking he doesn't like you. Fortunate is he who is able to make a friend of that enemy—and it's so easily done.

Several men who had taken a violent dislike to me, perhaps because of something I may have said in an unguarded moment, and would have liked figuratively to cut my throat, have become my staunchest friends merely by my thinking and believing that they were really friendly people.

I don't know where I got the idea of converting enemies into friends, whether it came to me out of the blue, whether I read it, or whether someone told me, but for years it has been part of my creed, and I've always found it to work. In illustration, let me tell the story of an executive who had taken a dislike to me for something I said critically about the operations of his company. For months, he was profanely "knocking me" at every opportunity. Naturally, my first impulse was to fight back and "knock" him in return. But the day came when I realized that his enmity had resulted from something I had said about *him* rather than the company, and I said to myself: "He's not a bad guy. I'm wrong. I started the feud, and I'm sorry. The next time I get near him I am going to tell him that mentally." One night I met him in a club of which we were both members. He would have avoided me, but we met nearly face to face, and I spoke first, saying, "How are you, Charlie?" He immediately responded and in the friendliest of manners. He caught "something" from my voice which meant a gesture of friendliness on my part, and today we're the closest of friends.

So remember this: some of our enemies may be of our own making. Those friends or enemies are merely a reflection of our own thoughts—the other fellow will consider us an enemy or friend according entirely to the picture which we ourselves conjure up.

Only today, as this is written, I had an example of this thought projection. The waste pipe of the laundry sink in my home had been clogged, and I had to call a plumber. A few blocks from our home was a plumbing shop, the proprietor of which was an unfriendly person and offensive in his treatment of customers. Several times I had tried to get him to do work for us, but he was always too busy.

The last time I had called him he had told me that I would have to wait my turn. Probably he could get around to fix up the water heater in a couple of weeks. I had asked him if he could give me the names of other plumbers who might help me, but he had been entirely unco-operative. Naturally, his unfriendly treatment had given me a bad impression of plumbers in general and I found myself damning all of them.

However, I had to get the heater repaired and I quickly realized that the angry attitude toward plumbers which had been engendered by this experience would cause me to have difficulty in obtaining the services of any one of them. I simply changed my thought, saying something like this to myself: "All plumbers are good fellows—the old guy you called is just an old grouch—forget it."

I had a friend, the manager of a wholesale plumbing house, and I called him to learn if he couldn't suggest a plumber who would help me. He did, and I telephoned him at once. He said he was busy, but if an imperative job had to be done, he would be out immediately. His promise pleased me and my gratitude for service was immediately felt by the plumber when he entered our home fifteen minutes after my call. In less than two hours—he worked swiftly, thus differing from some plumbers I had employed—the heater had been replaced. I was genuinely delighted by his service and told him so. That naturally pleased him.

Today it was a little before 8 A.M. when I called for help. I told the plumber who I was and reminded him that he had been the one who had fixed my water heater. He remembered me immediately and said that he'd be out just as soon as possible—probably around noon. Within five minutes after I had hung up the telephone receiver, a man appeared at the front door asking if I had called a plumber.

I asked him how it happened that he was on the job so soon when I had been told by his boss that he couldn't send a man before noon, and he replied, "Mr. ————— had just received your call as I came into the shop and he told me to come up to your home and do what was necessary before I went out on my all-day job."

I was elated with this treatment and told the plumber, which, of course, pleased him. With my help the necessary repairs on the waste pipe were made in less than half an hour. I told him of my previous experience with the old plumber and his own boss, and he replied:

"My boss is a fine fellow. He's always putting himself out to help people and he's building a huge business as a result. Never have I found a better boss."

You wager, think and believe that the other fellow is a fine chap, and that's what he'll turn out to be—for never forget that the thing we get back is a reflection of what we project mentally.

Do not reject this great truth. Just apply it and you'll be amazed at the startling results. Watch the bus driver respond, the elevator operator beam, and the clerk behind the counter hurry to oblige you when you send out friendly thoughts. It can be used in every encounter in life, and if you're wholly sincere about it, you will never have to worry about making enemies.

"And as ye would that men should do to you, do ye also to them likewise," says the Bible. As a matter of fact, many successful men and women, irrespective of any motive that may actuate them, work on the assumption that when they do something for the other person, something will be done for them. That may sound rather calculating, but the basic law of reciprocity remains, regardless of the situation or circumstances. It is simply that there must be a logical effect from every cause.

It isn't a matter of bootlicking when you try to please the boss. It's just common sense to make him a friend, for in any organization the people who get ahead are those who do their work well and try to please the boss. The boss is the man who does the promoting, and the more he is pleased with you and your work, the faster is your own progress. No matter how great your self-esteem, if you expect progress in any large organization, you must not only do your work well, but you must have the good will of the boss. Look around you a bit and you'll see this principle at work everywhere. You saw it work in the schoolroom when you were young, you saw it at work in the army, you see it in American politics, and if you have studied animal life you have recognized it working among the highest and the lowest types.

Take the initiative. Always try to do something for the other fellow and you will be agreeably surprised how things come your way—how many pleasant things are done for you. Doing something for others always pays dividends in one form or another.

You can experiment for yourself with your dog. Pet him and be kind to him, and his tail will wag in grateful appreciation and he will try to lick your hand or your face if you'll give him a chance. Scold him or strike him and he may cringe, snarl, or even attempt to bite you. The reactions of people are similar, and no matter what the motive may be that actuates you to do something for the other person, whether it be merely a friendly impulse or your own knowledge of the law of cause and effect, the results will be the same. Sincere compliments will always gain you friends, for most people are extremely susceptible to compliments. Compliments gratify their ego, and up you go in their friendly estimation. Successful politicians learn early in their careers the art of making friends by doing things for other people, and by speaking in praise of them. The corner newsboy you befriend today may some day be the judge before whom you stand when you have violated some traffic rule, and then you will discover what it means to have "a friend at court." The same principle applies in all walks of life, yet many people overlook the fact.

I sat in the office of the merchandise manager of one of the largest department stores in the country not long ago when a woman employee came in to thank him for some advice given her regarding the accepting of a better position with a firm in another city. When she left, he said:

"You know, one thing I like about this job is the number of people who come to me for advice. While you are aware that the job here keeps me on the jump, I always take time off for employees who come to me for advice. It flatters me and makes me feel as though I'm quite a fellow, and naturally I feel like doing everything I can for the people who so compliment me."

This brings me to another point—a person who desires riches must go where riches are. Alone on a desert island, a man would probably have a tough time eking out an existence, to say nothing of trying to amass a fortune. So it is in everyday pursuits. Therefore if you want money, you've got to associate yourself with people who have it or who know how to make it. This may sound rather gross. But the truth is that if it is money you are after, you must go where it is and where it is being spent, and also you must become personally acquainted with those who have the authority to spend it. If you are a salesman selling advertising and you know the head of the firm is the man with the final say, it's a waste of time trying to convince minor clerks and junior executives. The same holds true if you are trying to sell other commodities, or, what is more important, trying to sell yourself.

"If you work for a man, for goodness' sake work for him," said Elbert Hubbard, which brings me to a failing of many people with whom I have worked over a period of years—lack of interest in their jobs. They make no effort to learn anything outside the small sphere in which their jobs place them. Once I made a wager with the executive of a large concern whose name was frequently in the newspapers that I could find at least twenty people on his own local organization who had never heard of him, to say nothing of the position he occupied. He was nettled when he got the proof. Not only did he lose the bet, but his pride was hurt. Curiosity prompted me to check with other organizations that were nation-wide in their operations, and not a single employee could tell me the name of the head of the company or the street address of its main office.

This may sound unbelievable and even ridiculous to many readers. But if you have friends working in a minor capacity with some large institution, ask them the name of the treasurer or the senior vice-president of the concern. Unless the employee is an exception, the ignorance will surprise you. If you are a salesman for a major oil company or even a telephone operator, surely you should make some endeavor within a short time after your employment to learn the names of the men who head the company and something of their history. Yet it is surprising how many people accept positions and make no attempt to ascertain what the adjacent department manufactures or to learn anything about the company's general operations. Perhaps the heads of big organizations err in not carrying on educational campaigns for the benefit of employees. Of course, there are large corporations that have house organs containing the names of the executives, main office locations, and the like, and giving details about their method of operation. I talked with a woman employed by a large manufacturing plant who had been with the concern for many months, and outside of the name of the personnel manager who had employed her, she did not know the name of a single executive of the company in spite of the fact that the company's publication with articles written by various department heads went into her hands monthly.

The job you now hold is the steppingstone to the job above. How much do you know about it before you start moving toward it—just how much do you know about your company and its policies both inside and out? Many firms carry group insurance for their employees, with the employees paying a small part of the premiums. How many employees have ever read their policies? Few do, and, further, few know anything about their social security rights or what the various amounts taken from their payroll checks actually represent.

"Man is heir to the wisdom of the ages found within the covers of great books," remarked one of our great wise men, and yet it is surprising how many people never read a book, although the war did cause more people to seek the companionship of books. Strange as it may sound, few business men read anything besides the newspapers and a few trade journals, and when a check is made among professional men you find that they more or less limit themselves to books and literature dealing with their respective fields. I mention books, for no matter what the book may be—biography, fiction, history, or a scientific text—it is a rare book that doesn't contain an idea or two useful in your own work.

No one has a monopoly of knowledge, and yet we all know that knowledge is power when put to use. The greater the reader, the more his thinking is stimulated, and if he is a man of action, the more his efforts are accelerated.

Now is the right time to mention the highly interesting phenomenon of association of ideas and how one idea quickly links itself with another. This is of great value and should be cultivated by everyone, especially by a person engaged in creative work such as advertising, writing, selling or kindred lines.

For example, you see an automobile on a country road. Consider for a moment how many ideas can be derived from the mental picture of the automobile. It's made of steel, alloys and plastics—each furnishing major ideas that can be broken up into many others. Then we consider the wheels and tires—casings, the inner tubes, the valves—all bringing further association of ideas. We think of the roads over which they have traveled, and this suggests roads and their construction. Then we think of oil and gasoline, which brings further ideas through association, and before we know it we have started with an association of ideas that is seemingly endless.

Let's take a single idea in business. Suppose you are interested in the growth and sale of a new kind of nut. The first question naturally is: Can it be grown and sold at a profit? Naturally, by association of ideas you will be led to determine all matters dealing with the growth of the nut, the soil, location, climatic conditions, costs, labor problems; these will lead on to marketing programs, packaging, dealers who would be interested, brokers, shippers, and finally, the ultimate consumer. The field of ideas becomes enormous although association started with the thought of a single little nut.

A word should be said about packaging and eye-appeal, because here again we deal with the power of suggestion. Dealers in groceries, fruits, and garden vegetables know that even if there is no improvement in the products themselves, artistic, attractive-looking packages will bring a better price for the goods. You have only to stroll through a grocery store and note the articles which attract your attention to discover this fact for yourself. Excellence in packaging distinguishes the skilled chef from the ordinary restaurant cook. The expert chef knows the value of eye-appeal and accordingly arranges the food on the platters or plates to give it a more appetizing appeal, while the average cook, probably neither knowing nor caring, piles it on in any old fashion.

For several years I was interested in a celery farm. Prior to the interning of many Japanese during the war, my renter, an Italian, was always complaining that he could not compete with the Japanese and gave this as an excuse for his inability to fulfill his rent contracts. Intuitively, the Japanese knew the value of proper packaging. Their celery would be thoroughly washed, placed in new crates, and frequently, if sold in the form of hearts, would be attractively wrapped in paper carrying a boastful little message about the quality of the celery. My renter, a slovenly fellow, never, in my memory, washed a single bunch of celery. He placed it in second-hand crates and then he complained that his Japanese competitors were getting all the business.

Anyone who has traveled through the great farming belts of our country and Canada can tell by a glance at the house or barn whether the farmer is alive or whether he is dying on his feet. I think of some of the great orchardists of the Pacific Northwest who twenty or thirty years ago couldn't sell a whole wagonload of pears or apples for twenty dollars; and yet men who had the idea of attractive packaging and marketing in recent years have made large fortunes. It's nothing to get people to pay two dollars or more for a dozen apples or pears carefully wrapped in tissue, waxed paper, or tinfoil; some of these alert orchardists sell their products by mail to thousands of buyers throughout the world. I happen to know personally a number of these operators and their success in each instance has been predicated upon an idea that came to them in a flash and which developed as a result of their believing.

Now consider this matter of packaging in connection with yourself. Do you have eye-appeal? Do you wear clothes to give yourself the best appearance? Do you know the effect of colors and study those which best suit your form and temperament? Does your whole appearance set you apart from many who pass unnoticed in the crowd? If not, give thoughtful attention to personal packaging, for the world accepts you as you appear to be. Take a tip from the automobile manufacturers, the Hollywood make-up artists, or any of the great show producers, who know the value of eye-appeal and package their goods accordingly. When you have a combination of proper packaging and highest quality goods within the package, you have an unbeatable combination. The *you* within can do the same thing for the *you* outside—and you, too, have the unbeatable combination.

To satisfy yourself on what the right appearance will do for you, just pass by where there is construction under way. If you are well-dressed and have an air of prosperity and importance, workmen who may be in your path will step aside as you pass. Or you might try stepping into an outer office where others may be waiting to see a certain executive. Notice that the important-looking individual with the air and voice of authority gets first attention not only from the office attendants but from the executive.

No better example of the impressiveness of a good appearance can be given than the distinction made between individuals by attendants at a police station or jail. The stylishly dressed, well-poised business man is seldom ill-treated, while the man who has the appearance of a bum lands almost immediately in a cell. As a police reporter on metropolitan newspapers for a numbers of years, I saw this happen times without number. The fellow who looked as though he might be "somebody" and who had been arrested for a minor law infraction, often got a chair in the captain's office until he could telephone the judge or some friend to obtain his release, wnile the bum was carted off to jail, to get his release when and if he could.

The head of a huge automobile distributing agency told me that he was frequently called upon to close a sale with wealthy men who always bought the most expensive cars. "Not only do I take a shower," he said, "and change all my clothes, but I go to a barbershop and get everything from a shave to a shampoo and manicure. Obviously, it has something to do with my appearance, but further than that it does something to me inside. It makes me feel like a new man who could lick his weight in wildcats."

If you are properly attired when you are starting out on some important undertaking, you will feel within yourself that sense of power, which will cause people to give way before you and will even stir others to help you on your way. The right mental attitude, keeping your eyes straight ahead and fixed on your goal, throwing around you the proper aura, which is done by an act of your imagination or an extension of your personal magnetism, will work wonders, as Theos Bernard, in his *Penthouse of the Gods*, learned when he was cornered and stoned by a crowd of natives in Tibet. In his book he says that his first reaction was to fight, but the thought was immediately dismissed when he recalled that he had been taught to assume and maintain his own aura. Thus he straightened his shoulders, lifted high his head, directed his eyes straight ahead, and moved forward with a firm and rapid stride. Not only did the crowd give way, but others came forward and made a path for him.

A number of years ago I was on intimate terms with the chief of a large metropolitan fire department, a middle-aged man who seemed to fear nothing. His associates declared that the chief bore a charmed life. Once, in getting material for a personal story, I asked him if he thought he had a charmed life, and he laughed: "I don't know as you'd call it that. Maybe I'm somewhat of a fatalist, but I have never believed that I would be killed as long as I am chief. When I go into a place of danger, I always throw a white circle about myself, and nothing can come through that circle. It was a trick I learned from the Indians who lived near us when I was a kid. Maybe it's the worst kind of superstition, but that white aura has saved my life more times than I like to think about." He lived to be retired and died in his seventies from natural causes.

We all know the story of Babe Ruth, the great baseball player, and how "he called his shots." If he wanted to make a home run by batting the ball into right or left field, that's where he batted the ball. How he did this is perhaps known only to that great hero of all American boys, but surely it was uncanny. Against the mightiest pitchers he was able to bat the ball where he wanted, and his home-run record is something that will stand for a long time to come.

The name Ernie Pyle immediately brings to mind the premonition of death this famous war correspondent experienced before shipping out to the Pacific war. It will be poignantly recalled that the beloved Ernie had the feeling that when he left for the Pacific Theater of War, he would not return. On the contrary, there are many of the stories told by ex-servicemen who had the "feeling or belief" that even though frequently under intense fire, they were going to come through without being wounded—and come through they did.

You will find that many people subjected to great danger believe in the efficacy of this white-circle aura. Perhaps here again it is the result of the magic of believing. There are millions of automobile owners in this world who have a small disc in their automobiles which they believe will save them from accidents. But why stop with discs in automobiles?

The vibrations set up by others affect us much more than we realize, for we take on the characteristics of those with whom we are more or less constantly associated. It is well known that a man and wife frequently after long years of association grow to resemble one another and acquire many of the habits of one another. A baby will take on the emotional characteristics of the mother or the person who habitually cares for it, becoming susceptible to the fears, the likes and dislikes of the mother or the nurse, and frequently these emotional qualities remain for life. And the lovers of pets, especially of dogs, declare that the animals will take on some of the emotional characteristics of their owners—they will be ugly, friendly, happy, or quarrelsome, depending upon the emotional pattern of the person with whom they are most closely associated.

It is always important to remember that a negative person

can raise havoc in an organization or a home. The same amount of damage can be done by a strong negative personality as good can be done by a positive personality, and when the two are pitted against one another, the negative frequently becomes the more powerful. We all know what occasionally happens to a man living among uncivilized people—he goes native. Englishmen employed as plantation or mine operators in jungle outposts guard against this by shaving and meticulously dressing each evening for dinner.

An extremely nervous person in a position of authority can put nearly every person associated with him into a nervous state. You can see this happen in almost any office or shop where the executive is of a nervous type. Sometimes this emotional pattern will extend throughout an entire organization. After all, as has been said, an organization is only the extended shadow of the man who heads it. Thus, to have a smoothly running organization, all its members must be attuned to the thinking of the principal executive. A strong negative personality in such an organization, who is out of tune with the ideas of the management, can extend his negative vibrations to others and do great damage, just as one rotten apple in a box will soon cause all the others to rot. Likewise, one woman weeping can cause others in the same room to weep, one person laughing can cause others to laugh, and the yawn of a single person can cause an epidemic of yawns. We seldom realize how much our emotional vibrations affect others and how much we are affected by theirs.

If you would remain a positive type, avoid associating too much with anyone who has a negative or pessimistic personality. Many clergymen and personnel counselors often become victims of prolonged association with people who come to them with their troubles. The impact of the steady stream of woe and sorrow vibrations eventually reverses their positive polarity and reduces them to a negative state.

To get a better understanding of the effect of these suggestive vibrations, you need only remember your varying feelings upon entering different offices or homes. The atmosphere, which is the creation of the people habitually frequenting the office or home, can be instantly detected as being upsetting, disturbing, tranquil, or harmonious.

You can tell almost instantly whether the atmosphere is

cold or warm—the arrangement of the furniture, the color scheme, the very walls themselves, all vibrate to the thinking of the persons occupying the place, and bespeak the type to which their thoughts belong. Whether the home be a mansion or a shack, the vibrations are always a key to the personality of those who occupy it.

Are you afraid to take on responsibilities, afraid to make decisions, afraid to step out alone? Most people are—that's why there are so few leaders and so many followers. If you are confronted with a problem, the longer you put it off, the greater it becomes and the more fearful you become of your ability to solve it. Therefore, learn to make decisions, because in not deciding you fail to act, and in failing to act you invite failure. Experience will soon teach you that once a decision is made, the problems and troubles begin to disappear. Even though the decision you make may not be the best one, the mere deciding gives you strength and raises your morale. It's the fear of doing the wrong thing that attracts the wrong thing. Decide and act, and the chances are that your troubles will fade into thin air—whether you make a mistake or not. All great men are men of quick decision which flows from their intuition, their accumulated knowledge, and previous experience. So learn to be quick in making decisions and audacious in your actions.

The writer makes no claim to being a faith-healer, but anyone who knows anything about the power of mind knows of the effects that emotionalized thinking has upon the condition of the body and knows also what suggestion can do toward bringing disease, as well as curing it. In some faith-healing movements, cures are affected by denying that the disease exists, and there are thousands who attest to the validity of this method of healing. Followers of other schools of healing make no attempt to deny the existence of disease, but instead ignore it, affirming that they are well and happy and getting better every day. Members of the various schools of thought are the best judges of the methods that work best for them; but it must be remembered that in all cases it is the individual's belief that determines the success of the individual method of cure. However, it is interesting to note that the movement which advocates denial has a tremendous following, and its membership continues to increase by leaps and bounds.

Just how far suggestion can be used to cure disease or physical ailments is still a matter of great controversy among the various schools of mental healing and members of the medical profession, but the fact remains that there are many thousands in our country alone—and the number increases daily—who are of the firm belief that a cure of their ailments came as result of mental-healing.

It has long been known that the emotions developed by fear, hate, and worry can lead to many bodily ills, even to fatal illnesses, although there are still some members of the medical profession who refuse to acknowledge this fact. However, *Life* magazine (February 19, 1945), in an article entitled "Psychosomatic Medicine," declared that during the war period it was found that 40 per cent of all army disability cases originated from psychosomatic causes. ("Psychosomatic" refers to a combination of mind and body ailments brought on by the emotions, and the prescribed treatment is a combination of psychotherapy and medical treatment.) The article pointed out that many cases of hay fever, bronchial asthma, heart disease, high blood pressure, rheumatic disease, arthritis, diabetes mellitus, the common cold, and various skin conditions such as warts, hives, and allergic reactions, were caused either by emotional upsets directly or by physical disturbances in which the emotions were an aggravating factor. The treatment consists of locating the source of the emotional disturbances and endeavoring to eradicate it.

Because of the experiments of the psychiatrists and psychoanalysts during the war, the whole subject of both medical and mental treatment is probably due for a complete revision, with resulting mind-cures which may prove astounding.

However, those who understand the science of psychotherapeutics are fairly well agreed that a cure does not come through treatment on the part of the healer nearly so much as it does from the patient himself. In other words, the suggestion, no matter in what form it is given by the healer (whether in accordance with the principles of psychotherapeutics or in conjunction with some special religious belief), is in turn transmitted by autosuggestion to the patient's own subconscious mind where it becomes effective. The writer realizes that the following statement may invite criticism, but the fact remains that if a patient refuses to believe in the suggestive appeals of the healer, the purpose is never accomplished. The two, the healer and the patient, have to be *en rapport* to get results, and it is the writer's theory that any person who possesses an understanding of the use of the power of suggestion could get the same results without the aid of a healer, provided he were sufficiently strong and constant in his own convictions and suggestions. The same technique, the cards and the mirror, with suitable affirmations, can be used to great advantage.

In recent years there has been a renewed interest in telepathy or thought-transference, arising out of the experiments and investigations carried on in many colleges and universities, particularly those conducted under the direction of Dr. J. B. Rhine of Duke University. Of course, Joseph Dunninger, radio's self-styled mentalist, with his so-called feats of thought-projection as well as mind-reading, has done much to widen popular discussion of the subject.

The records of both the American and British Societies for Psychical Research are filled with case reports of telepathy, clairvoyance, and similar phenomena, but many people, despite the published reports of scientific findings, are prone to scoff at the idea that telepathy exists.

It has always struck the writer as odd that many people who profess to believe in the Bible, in which there are countless stories of visions, clairvoyance, and telepathy, declare that today telepathy and kindred phenomena are not possible.

Notwithstanding the general skepticism, some of the world's greatest scientific thinkers have declared that telepathy is not only possible but that it is a faculty that can be used by most people when they understand it. In addition to the findings of both the American and British Societies for Psychical Research and the results made public by Dr. Rhine, there are numerous old and new books on the subject. A few of the better known ones are *Mental Radio,* by Upton Sinclair; *Beyond the Senses,* by Dr. Charles Francis Potter, well-known New York preacher; *Thoughts Through Space,* by Harold Sherman and Sir Hubert Wilkins, famous explorer; *Telepathy,* by Eileen Garrett, editor and publisher; and *Experimental*

Telepathy, by René Warcollier, Director of The Institute Metaphysique International, in Paris.

When the results of Dr. Rhine's experiments at Duke University were first made public, there were many men who rushed into print to declare that the results could be laid to chance, and considerable time and money were spent in an endeavor to prove that telepathy was non-existent. Yet the experiments continue at Duke and at other leading universities. The writer has often wondered why many opposing so-called scientific investigators do not try to prove that the phenomena exist instead of trying to prove the contrary; but here again the writer has a theory that belief is the miracle worker, and this is partly substantiated by what Dr. Rhine himself says in his book on extrasensory perception. He declares that satisfactory results were secured when the experimenters caught the "spirit of the thing," and that the ability to transmit and receive became weakened when the original novelty wore off. In other words, while there was enthusiasm there was spontaneous interest and the belief that it could be done. But when students were called back at later dates to continue their experiments in the course of their studies, enthusiasm was lacking, and the results were not satisfactory.

Perhaps many of my readers will recall an article which appeared in the *American Weekly* magazine, August 25, 1946, captioned "Scientific Evidence Man Has a Soul," written by Dr. J. B. Rhine. In view of the fact that his explanations deal directly with the subject matter of this book, I quote the article almost in full.*

What has science to say about the soul? For the answer to this question we would naturally turn to psychology because it is literally "the science of the soul." But here we have a surprise coming to us, for we find that the soul theory of man has been practically dropped from psychology books and lectures.

Most psychologists will even smile tolerantly if one speaks of the mind itself as if there were such a thing apart from the brain. Everything has to be physical to be

_____

*Reprinted by courtesy of the author, Dr. J. B. Rhine, and with the permission of *The American Weekly*.

real, according to the prevailing view; anything non-physical or spiritual, as the soul is supposed to be, therefore simply cannot be. Such an idea has to be dismissed as pure superstition.

The principles of physics are expected to explain everything that we call "mental," if they continue to expand as they have been doing.

However, some things occur now and then that just do not fit in at all with this physical view of man. For example, a person may awaken from a horrible dream in which a friend or relative is dying. The shocking picture turns out to be essentially true and the timing about right, although the friend may be a thousand miles away.

The oddest feature of all this is that in some cases the event perceived may not occur until hours or days after the dream; yet it may have been accurately pictured and even experienced in considerable detail.

The first thought is, of course, that such experiences are mere coincidences. Not many people get beyond this first easy explanation, but fortunately a few have done so; and when one studies great numbers of these experiences, they lose all appearance of being accidental. The scientific thing to do, of course, was to set to work to discover what might lie behind these happenings.

Obviously if any of these "psychic" experiences showed that the mind has the power to reach out beyond space and time, they would plainly be transcending physical law. The mind would then be demonstrated to be a spiritual rather than a physical system. Here was a clue to the soul. Just a clue—nothing more; but it provided the necessary lead to reliable evidence.

It was from these "psychic" experiences that the ESP tests were derived. ESP is the abbreviation of extrasensory perception, which includes telepathy and clairvoyance. In other words, telepathy and clairvoyance are two different modes of acquiring knowledge without the use of the recognized sense organs such as the eyes and ears. In a typical telepathy test the person being tested tries to identify which card or number or other symbol is being held in mind by another person—who is, let us say, located in an adjoining room. In a clairvoyance test, on the other hand, it is the object itself, commonly a card, instead of the thought of it, which the percipient tries to perceive. In a word, telepathy is the ESP of the state of mind of another person; clairvoyance, the ESP of an object.

At Duke University in 1930 a small group of psychologists began a series of ESP experiments of both types, telepathy and clairvoyance. This work was sponsored by the great British psychologist, William McDougall, Fellow of the Royal Society, who was at the time the head of the Department of Psychology at Duke. This work which was carried out in what came to be called the Parapsychology Laboratory ("para" meaning the unusual, the exceptional, the unorthodox) was by no means the first of its kind. Experiments had been done here and there, some of them even in universities, for as much as fifty years before, but there had been no systematic, consecutive experimentation following up the problems through the years, such as took place at Duke. That university was the first to offer a permanent haven to active research on "psychic" problems.

The experimenters in the Parapsychology Laboratory found fresh confirmatory evidence of both types of ESP, telepathic and clairvoyant. They developed and standardized new tests, making it easier to repeat the experiments. This had the effect of starting a movement of ESP experimentation which spread to many other institutions here and abroad. Elaborate precautions were taken to insure that no sensory cues were possible and that no other type of error could affect the test results. The tests were of such a nature that the scores could be evaluated by standard and long-approved statistical methods. It could be shown clearly that the scores made in the tests could not reasonably be accounted for, either by chance or by experimental weakness of any kind.

Once the experimenters were satisfied that the occurrence of ESP was soundly established, they set to work on the vitally important question as to what relation that capacity had to the physical world. Do telepathy and clairvoyance operate strictly under physical law? Or do they reach beyond the limits of physics as the spontaneous "psychic" experiences seem to do?

Fortunately it was a simple matter to test ESP in relation to space. For example, we needed only to conduct tests with long distance between the cards and the person trying to identify them by ESP, and compare the results with short-distance tests. Both telepathy and clairvoyance tests gave as good results at great distances as they did with small. Distance measured in yards, miles, or hundreds of miles simply did not matter in the operation of ESP, as far as the experiments went. For that matter, angles, barriers, and other physical conditions seemed likewise to have no effect on success in the ESP tests.

What, then, about time? We argued that if space does not influence ESP, time should not be expected to affect it either. The tests for ESP of the future, or precognition (prophecy is a more familiar word), were easily derived from the regular ESP tests. People who could successfully identify cards extrasensorially at a distance were then asked to try to predict what the order of cards was going to be after the deck was shuffled. We found that they scored as well on decks of cards that were mechanically shuffled before checking as they did trying to identify the cards as they were in the deck at the time. Moreover, they did as well at predicting the order of the deck of cards ten days ahead as for a two-day period. Length of time beyond the prediction and the check-up following the shuffling made no more difference than had the length of distance in the earlier experiments.

There was only one interpretation of these experiments possible—namely, that the mind of man somehow transcends the space-time limitations of the physical world in these capacities we are calling "extrasensory perception." As the experiments were confirmed by other research men and women in other laboratories, the conclusion became firmly established that the mind does indeed possess properties not belonging to physics as we know it. Since space and time are the surest indications of what is physical, the mind must, therefore, be extraphysical or spiritual in nature. And all we mean by the

"soul" in man is that the mind is nonphysical—or spiritual—in character. The ESP experiments, then, have yield-
ed evidence of the soul in man.

To some people this will seem a very small beginning
on the problem of the soul. Certainly we must not
exaggerate the extent of the findings. Actually we have
done little more than produce evidence for an elemental
sort of soul theory. There is, of course, a great deal more
to the religious concept of the soul than has been found
in these researches. There are many great problems
remaining. Is the soul capable of separation from the
body? Can it survive bodily death? If it can and does, can
discarnate souls have any contact with the living, or in
any way influence them? What about the idea of a
world-soul, or God? What about communication between
souls, especially the soul of man and God? These and
many other fundamental questions of religious doctrine
remain untouched by anything thus far discussed in this
article.

All we have a right to conclude is that the physical
concept of man which has increasingly prevailed in
intellectual circles since the rise of materialism is now
thoroughly disproved.

There is something—how much, we do not know—
definitely extraphysical about humans.

There is an order of reality in human life not subject
to the laws of time and space.

But it is just as important, I think, to recognize, too,
the tremendous possibilities we can now see. The soul-
theory of man gives us much to build on in our further
thinking on religious problems. We have now verified the
essential foundation upon which the spiritual philosophy
of man was originally erected. It remains for scientific
inquiry to go on further to find out by the same methods
all we can about human personality, its nature and
destiny—in short, to take up the other great questions of
religion.

There was a time when experimental inquiry into the
problems of religion would have met with vigorous opposition from orthodox religious leaders. There are still
many conservatives that would resent the intrusion of

science into the domain of what they think should be pure faith. But a great many of the most deeply religious men and women of today are eagerly reaching out for a more tangible sort of knowledge regarding the human mind and all of its potentialities that lie far beyond our present knowledge.

Surprisingly enough, it has been from orthodox science that we have met with the main opposition. The scientific conservative especially fears any division in nature, any such dualism as that of soul and body—so much so that he is likely to refuse to look at any evidence which suggests such a duality. Such anxiety is quite groundless, for if, as we may now claim to know, man does have a soul as well as a body, both fundamentally different, the two are still in some sense unified.

They do interact; therefore they have something in common. Two things cannot affect each other if they differ in every single point. We see, therefore, that there must be a world of hidden realities, probably neither physical nor mental as we know them, from which the manifestations of mind and body, the psychical and physical, orginally stem. This realm beyond mind and matter lies there almost as unknown as the American continents were to Columbus, silently awaiting some fortunate explorer of the future. But he will have to be someone who, like the great Genoese sailor, was daring enough to question existing charts of knowledge and belief—and put them to experimental test.

The writer has frequently attended séances at which the medium has refused to perform, declaring that someone in the audience was a scoffer, a nonbeliever, whose vibrations were creating a hostile atmosphere. The materialistic skeptic may laugh at this, but the writer has been present at large meetings where one lone heckler in the audience with his persistent hostility has not only disrupted the meeting, but completely defeated the efforts of the speaker.

I think that anyone who understands the vibratory theory of thought power can also understand why unsympathetic vibrations can be "monkey wrenches thrown into the machinery." Verification of this is found in the experiments by

Dr. Rhine, who discovered in his psychokinesis tests that when a subject operated in the presence of an observer who tried to distract him and depress his scoring, the results were always below expectancy. And, contrariwise, when the same subject performed alone or in the presence of neutral or sympathetic observers, his score of successes was correspondingly high.

You have only to read the story of witchcraft, the story of voodoo medicine men and "hexers," and even the achievements of present-day mental-healers to realize that there is undoubtedly some force at work which influences others even at a distance. True, the suggestion first planted in the mind of the patient or victim, as the case may be, has for its purpose either good or evil; but that doesn't account for the results, especially in the absent-treatment method where the patient may have no knowledge that the healer is "working" on him. Whether telepathy is involved here is something that has not yet been established.

It is to be noted that practically all of the great electrical scientists, including Edison, Steinmetz, Tesla, and Marconi, were greatly interested in telepathy. Dr. Alexis Carrel not only believed in telepathy but declared that a study of it should be made by scientific men, just as physiological phenomena are studied.

Despite the fact that the secretary of the London Society for Psychical Research after twenty years of investigation by its members stated that telepathy is an actuality, and the further fact that experiments at the various colleges continue to pile up amazing evidence of its existence, there are many scientific men who refuse to accept the findings. Moreover, the number of people who are carrying on investigations of their own is constantly growing, even though they are regarded in certain quarters as being eccentric and somewhat gullible. I have often wondered if those who belittle this research work are really being fair, both to themselves and those interested in the phenomena, especially when the research work may lead to greater discoveries than hitherto dreamed possible.

Many horse and dog fanciers, especially those who have kept horses and dogs as pets over a long period of years, stoutly maintain the existence of telepathy between the animals and themselves, and there have been countless stories told regarding telepathic phenomena among primitive people in all parts of the world.

Long years ago a business executive told me that he got rid of people who were taking up his time by simply repeating mentally to his visitor: "It's time for you to go, leave now, leave now." The visitor would shortly get fidgety, look at his watch or get up from his chair, reach for his hat, and soon be on his way out.

You can get the same results when visitors overstay their time in your home. When you feel it is time for them to go, simply say to yourself, "Go home now, go home now, go home now," and you will find that they glance around the room looking for the clock and say, "Guess it's about time we were leaving."

I recognize that some skeptics say that telepathy has nothing to do with this, that your facial expressions, your bodily movements, signs of nervousness or weariness are what warn the visitor that it is time for him to leave. However, experiment for yourself; but take care that you give the visitor no outward sign, either by word or facial expression, that it is time for his departure. You will find that there are times, especially if the visitor is intent upon putting over a point or winning an argument, that this procedure will not work. But the moment there is a lull in the conversation, try it and the results will astonish you.

A number of years ago I had my office on the second floor of a large office building. In later years the firm with which I had been associated moved to the tenth floor. Often upon entering the elevator I would say, "Ten, please," to the operator, and then immediately begin thinking about the second floor and of its various associations in connection with my work. Time after time I found the elevator operator, who didn't know me or my earlier association, stopping at the second floor and then turning around to look at me.

A well-known Pacific Coast clergyman who was a deep student of Mind Stuff told me that every time he wanted flowers in his church, he simply sent his thoughts out to members of his congregation and someone would send flowers. He also told me that every memorial window in his church came as a result of the mental suggestions which he gave whenever he felt the time was propitious for another window.

Dr. Roy Chapman Andrews, in a radio program in April, 1945, told of one of the most unusual "coincidences" on record. He related the story of an American song writer who just after the publication of one of his songs discovered that the same piece of music, note for note, had been composed in Germany only a short time previously. The fact that the compositions to the last note were identical makes the story more unusual than the many cases that have been reported of widely separated people who have had the same idea at the same time. The writer, living on the West Coast, submitted a short time before this book was written an article to an eastern publication only to receive a note from the editor saying an article embracing the same material had just been accepted from another writer living in the East. Elisha Gray claimed that he had the idea of the telephone at the same time as Alexander Graham Bell. Independent simultaneous discovery of ideas often happens among writers, inventors, chemists, engineers, and composers.

Even during the preparation of this book, when suggestions were being made for changes and additions, both my agent-adviser and myself were often surprised to learn that we both received ideas at almost identical times. Not only did we get similar ideas, but the suggestive use of identical names of people came to us almost simultaneously. Early when my publishers suggested additional matter, I had been engaged in research work for a week when I received a letter from my adviser stating that he had suggested to the publisher the identical subject matter on which I had been working. Checking disclosed that the same thoughts had come to us at approximately the same time. Naturally, there is no way of knowing whether my adviser in New York caught my thoughts or whether I caught his. I merely report the facts.

CHAPTER VIII

Women and the Science of Belief

As IDEAS for this book occurred to me, I frequently thought of the many famous women who had used the power of belief, and once in discussion with Ben Hur Lampman, nationally known author and naturalist, he suggested that I specifically cover its use by women, saying:

"Many women, perhaps, may not realize that they can use your science just as advantageously as men, and you should be specific in your message to them. Once they understand and apply what you give, they'll find themselves in a position figuratively to turn the world upside down. If there were some way for women of all nationalities to unite and use this science, there would be no future wars.

"Women are supreme egotists—in the sense that when they get the idea they can do something, and that idea becomes thoroughly imbedded in their consciousness, they will stop at nothing to achieve their purpose. You know the old saying, 'The female of the species is more deadly than the male.' That is true, and once women understand their power —and you can give them the clue—nothing will stop them. If they wish, they may actually run this old world. 'Heaven has no rage like love to hatred turned, nor hell a fury like a woman scorned,' and once they are aroused and understand what they can accomplish there will be no stopping them. Women are more versatile, more adaptable. Even though Napoleon declared that he made circumstances, most men are its victims, while women by their very nature of thinking make circumstances serve them."

Then when I read an article by a woman complaining that American women "don't get a break," it dawned on me that if women of today "don't get a break," it is the fault of no one but themselves. The only thing they have to do is to follow the examples of their sisters who have preceded them and have made their own "breaks."

Therefore, I want to emphasize the importance of the adoption of this science by women for their own special needs, and in the following pages I shall give examples of women in the past and present who have used it with great effectiveness. Let us realize that when woman awakens, she is going to play a more vital part than ever in the affairs of the world.

As a matter of fact, even today American women, although they may not be aware of it, are potentially in a position to have things pretty much their own way, for they actually control the wealth of this country!

During the war, we had women welders, women riveters, the Wacs, Waves, and Spars, and they all had a taste of actually performing tasks heretofore handled only by men. To thousands of single girls and housewives who had never had an opportunity to do anything outside the home, those experiences should have pointed out their own potential opportunities for taking a more active part in the work of this world.

In our own country today there are thousands of outstanding women—from great educators to bankers and industrialists, to say nothing of the numerous writers, editors, and other professional women. Many of the greatest reforms in America have been the ideas of women; if the facts could be assembled, it could easily be proven that not only did the ideas for these great reforms originate with women, but the women were the driving force behind the ideas. Some male readers may resent these statements, but there is no escaping the facts.

As a former newspaper man, naturally I had to follow the feminist movement, and for nearly forty years I have seen and felt the power of outstanding women.

When it was first suggested that I emphasize the use of this science for women, I immediately thought of Mrs. R. E. Bondurant, who has been active in women's work, charities, the inauguration of child labor laws, the building of homes and hospitals for delinquent girls, numerous legislative measures to further the interest of women and children, and public movements to aid the blind and other handicapped people. Her nationally known record of nearly forty years is an outstanding one, and today at seventy-one, even though perhaps a partial cripple for the rest of her life, she is just as enthusiastic as ever and is seeking new worlds to conquer.

Of late years, Mrs. Bondurant has been an ardent worker in the cause of the Chin-Uppers, an organization consisting of blind, crippled, and otherwise partly disabled men and women. Now she is planning to open a store where articles made by these people may be sold. In this she has the co-operation of a number of business men. Mrs. Bondurant told me that if necessary she was going to pay the rent out of her own pocket, but that all the profit would go to the Chin-Uppers. I spent a Sunday afternoon with her in her sitting-room among her books and flowers. A pair of crutches stood in a corner near the door. (For months Mrs. Bondurant has had to use them, but even at her advanced age she gets around on trolley cars, buses, and in and out of automobiles without help.) Although today she uses a cane when she leaves her home, in my presence she moved around the room without limping. We discussed at length this matter of believing. Mrs. Bondurant said:

There is no question about it, and I can speak from a pretty full life of seventy-one years, during which time I not only raised a family but have taken part in the various movements and activities with which you have long been familiar. There is certainly something, call it a power, God, or anything you wish, which is always there to sustain us in time of need. I have never seen it fail. We've just got to believe and when I look back through the years and recall the fine women with whom I was associated when we were working for legislation to bring about better working conditions for women and children, I realized that it was the "indomitable spirit" of these women, who thoroughly believed in the righteousness of their cause, that made the legislation possible and effective.

I am astounded at the fact that the average woman doesn't realize her tremendous power. I don't call it stupidity because I would never admit that women are stupid, but rather they lack interest. I am amazed, in talking to women's groups, to realize that many of them never knew that these great reform movements to help them and their children were initiated by women, and it is my opinion that once women become aware of their strength and power, they can do more to bring about lasting peace and make this world a better place in which to live than all the famous male warriors and would-be peacemakers. All the great forward movements, as a matter of fact, I might say, all the great things in this world, have been done by men and women who were dreamers and believers in their dreams coming true. They could not have accomplished things otherwise. It's like the old story about climbing to the top of the mountain in search of that indefinable something. It makes no difference from which side the approach is made, those who steadfastly climb reach the top, and so it is with this matter of believing. It isn't so much what the real or imaginary object of our belief may be, it's the belief and following through that makes the thing possible.

I don't want to appear critical, but it has been my observation that people don't have sufficient action or driving force behind their beliefs. For example, some women's organizations will pass resolutions in favor of or against this and that, and think that settles the matter. The resolutions are no good unless the sentiments expressed are actually brought to the attention of the powers that be.

I don't know of any greater thing in life than the satisfaction that comes through serving. During the many years I spent in sponsoring the various causes and getting legislation adopted, I never received a penny in pay or to cover my expenses. While it may sound like Pollyanna business to many people, bread tossed upon the waters does come back. In illustration, I might tell you that during the depression my husband lost $80,000. He was sick in bed at home and I would go to the office daily to get the mail and check the routine. Sometimes it looked as if we would not have sufficient money to meet imperative needs, but just about when we had to meet the obligations, checks would appear in the mail from people to whom Mr. Bondurant had lent money or from long-overdue accounts. We had some pretty hard times those days, but help always came through just in time and I never lost my belief.

As I watched and listened to Mrs. Bondurant, I realized that I was in the presence of no ordinary woman, but rather of a human dynamo who had the spirit and determination to get things done through her great belief. When I recalled that she had been credited with having had more laws in the interest of women and children passed than any other woman or organization in the state, I realized what it would mean to the world if all women with her vision and driving force undertook to use this science.

In the news not so long ago were found the stories a few weeks apart of the passing of two great women, one of whom was Grace Moore, she with the beautiful singing voice, and the other, that fiery British woman leader, Miss Ellen Wilkinson. Both women knew early in life what they wanted.

In common with a great many men and women who have reached great heights, Grace Moore won her success in the face of difficulties that would have stopped even some of the strongest men. As a child, she dreamed of becoming a great opera singer. The little girl went out to win the hearts of people everywhere. Even as a penniless runaway in New York, where often she had to sing for her supper in small Greenwich Village cafés, Grace Moore never lost her courage. She made her debut at seventeen and was close to the zenith of her career at forty-five. Again and again when it appeared that she was hopelessly defeated, she, with unquenchable courage, emerged victorious. When she lost her voice and was told by a throat specialist she would never sing again, she put up a tremendous battle, and emerged from a year of retirement and rest, singing more beautifully than ever before. Her glorious voice brought her great fame, and up to the time of her unfortunate death in the airplane crash at Copenhagen early in 1947, Grace Moore continued to believe in her dreams.

She was one of the few stars who believed in helping other talented people to achieve their objectives and her timely aid assisted many unknown aspiring singers. When one of her protégées who had achieved success became temperamental about her part in a performance, it is said that Miss Moore told her that a famous singer had once advised her that to great artists there was no such thing as a small part and to small artists there were no big parts.

Ellen Wilkinson, who was the British Minister of Education, was a tiny, red-haired woman who drove her way upward through her persistence. Less than five feet tall, she was never cowed by the biggest of the British leaders. It is said that she made a career of annoyance, first as a school teacher, then as a suffragist, a novelist, newspaper writer, and finally cabinet minister. She was pleased when someone said of her that no woman in the whole of Britain had been more active, more persistent, or more annoying. Probably her greatest contribution in the interest of the people was her campaign to raise the age of leaving school from fourteen to fifteen. She won this fight in the face of stiff opposition of fellow ministers and the great demand for youths in British industry.

From the time of Cleopatra to the present, there have been thousands of women who, relying on their inmost convictions, have had a direct hand in shaping the lives of millions. It has been said that behind every great ruler was a woman. This may not be historically correct, but certainly we have enough evidence to know that women have had very much of a guiding hand in history-making. The names of several women who achieved success through their beliefs come to mind.

One was Empress Eugénie who married Napoleon the Third. When a small child she had fallen against a bannister and bruised her body. Her gypsy nurse told her not to cry, that she would be a queen and live to be a hundred. She believed in gypsies and her fortune materialized nearly as prophesied. She became Empress Eugénie and lived until she was ninety-four, just six years less than the age fixed by her gypsy nurse.

Madame Marie Curie, the famous co-discoverer of radium, was told when a child in Warsaw by an old gypsy woman that she would be famous. The story is that Marja Skłodowska, later to be known as Madame Curie, was running to join a group of playmates when the old gypsy woman stopped her, demanding that the girl show her hand. The other children did not want Marja to listen to the gypsy, but the gypsy woman held on to the little hand, excitedly commenting on the remarkable lines in her palm and telling the child she would be famous. As we all know, Madame Curie became one of the most famous women of modern times.

The desire to discover what lay behind that strange phenomenon all around us known as radioactivity, literally drove Professor Pierre Curie and Marie, his wife, to the epochal discovery of radium. Whether or not the words of the old gypsy fortune-teller inspired Madame Curie and influenced her career, perhaps history will never know. But as one reads about her life, that conclusion would appear to be an obvious one, for early in her girlhood Madame Curie made up her mind to become a scientist. When she was refused permission to study science at the University of Cracow (the secretary told her that women should not concern themselves with science, and suggested that she enter cookery classes), she went to Paris and entered the Sorbonne, supporting herself by teaching and working in the laboratories. It was there she met Pierre Curie and, once embarked with him on the task of tracking down at least one source of radioactivity, nothing stopped her. She had two daughters, a household to manage, as well as the problem of combatting ill health, but she refused to give up her laboratory work even when her husband begged her to. Few women have been so greatly honored as Madame Curie, the woman who was told by an old gypsy that some day she would be famous. Madame Curie certainly made those childhood prophecies come true.

An amazing story, perhaps one of the strangest on record and one proving further that there is great power in believing, is found in that of Opal Whiteley. This astounding historical case clearly shows that, as pointed out by William James, belief creates its verification in fact; it affords unmistakable proof that often events are influenced by our very great desires.

This is the story of a girl who, according to those who knew her in her childhood, was the daughter of an American family named Whiteley, the head of which was an Oregon logger. She, however, believed herself to be the daughter of Henri d'Orléans, heir to the Bourbon claim to the Crown of France. She was credited with having written a diary supposed to have been compiled when she was six or seven years of age, which told about her "angel" father and "angel" mother of royal blood; this was printed in 1920 under the auspices of the *Atlantic Monthly*. It created a sensation and precipitated a big literary controversy. Drawn into the controversy were psychologists, scientists, astrologers, psychics, editors, clergymen, literary critics, and almost every person who had at any time known Opal.

In Alfred Powers' *History of Oregon Literature*, there is a chapter by Elbert Bede, in which Mr. Bede says: "I haven't the least doubt that a large part of Opal's diary is a hoax and a large part plagiarism, and I have presented facts that show the foster parentage claim impossible."

The diary was printed when Opal was about twenty-two years of age, and even though Opal Whiteley may not have been born of Indian royalty, she was actually accepted as such in later years.

In 1933, some thirteen years after her diary had been printed, the newspapers carried a story about an American woman traveling in India. While she was in the state of Udaipur, she had a remarkable experience. She was sitting in her carriage, when she was astounded to see another carriage led by a half troop of cavalry coming toward her. In the other carriage was Opal Whiteley, the girl from the logging camp of Oregon, and later investigators disclosed that Opal Whiteley was actually residing in the household of the Maharaja of Udaipur, the ruling Indian prince. The same newspaper stories told how Ellery Sedgwick, editor of the *Atlantic Monthly* when her diary was printed, verified the story that the girl was actually residing in the royal household. They further related that Mr. Sedgwick had received from the secretaries of two maharajas' courts substantiation of this story, and in his book, *The Happy Profession*, Mr. Sedgwick has a chapter devoted to this strange tale.

I have had several talks with Mr. Bede, who for many years was a well-known Oregon newspaper man, and is now editor of the *Oregon Mason*, regarding the remarkable way in which Opal molded her destiny, and Mr. Bede said to me: "*It was uncanny, almost supernatural, the manner in which circumstances suited themselves to her plans.*"

Mr. Bede, like most people who knew the girl in her

childhood, is absolutely convinced that Opal was born of
American parents, the Whiteleys. He told me that he had
known her quite well and that she had frequently been in his
home in Cottage Grove. "My first knowledge of Opal came
when I was reporting a Junior Christian Endeavor convention
in Cottage Grove, and I was informed that a seventeen-year-
old girl from a near-by logging camp had been elected
president. My first impression of Opal was that of a vibrant,
fluttery, exotic, whimsical person, informed strangely beyond
her years, eager, deeply earnest, and seriously religious. She
later became to me an inexplicable enigma.

"She was always planning, always planning well in advance
anything she would undertake. It was most amazing how, in
preparation of a nature book, *The Fairyland Around Us*,
which she was writing, she could solicit contributions from
such persons as Andrew Carnegie and John D. Rockefeller,
and actually got money from some of them. A leaflet advertising the book carried expressions of wondering admiration
from such persons as Queen Elizabeth of Belgium, Theodore
Roosevelt, Nicholas Murray Butler, Gene Stratton Porter,
and others of equal prominence."

I was struck by this paragraph in Mr. Bede's story: "With
all these plans so well laid so long before the jaunt of Opal to
Massachusetts' center of culture, I have often wondered what
plans she had made to give the diary to the publishers. And
then how Ellery Sedgwick should accidentally ask for the
diary."

As I studied these words, I wondered if it was really an
accident that Mr. Sedgwick should ask for the diary and if
this strange girl had not "telepathically" given the thought to
Mr. Sedgwick. I did not discuss this point with Mr. Bede, but
if Opal Whiteley knew how mentally to transmit her thoughts
to others in advance, then it explains how Mr. Sedgwick
happened to ask if she had kept a diary.

For years I have carried the conviction that people close to
nature and those intimately associated with both wild and
domesticated animals have an understanding or an insight that
enables them to see far beyond the horizons of most ordinary
folks who live in the cities and never get nearer to a cow than
a milk bottle. I have always believed that to these people
nature reveals many of her secrets which are withheld from

those who live in penthouses in our modern cities. Whether or not telepathy, or the ability to transmit our thoughts silently so that others catch them, is one of the secrets which nature reveals to those close to her, is something I cannot answer, although it is common knowledge that jungle dwellers and savages in all quarters of the world know the secret of telepathy and have used it for centuries. There are numerous books on telepathy among primitives; as a famous editor once said to me, "To accept the idea that these natives don't use it would put us in the class of the uninformed."

Now let's review what Mr. Bede had to say about Opal and her closeness to nature.

"A volume would hardly suffice to summarize the personality of the nature-tutored child, who had at the age of six, so her diary would have us believe, confided her most intimate secrets to Michael Angelo Sanzio Raphael (a fir tree), and whose associates instead of people were Lars Porsena of Clusium (a crow), Thomas Chatterton Jupiter Zeus (a most dear wood rat), Brave Horatius (a shepherd dog), Peter Paul Rubens (a pet pig), and other characters with equally classical appellations.

"In her adolescent years, Opal gathered geological specimens, and bugs and worms by the thousands, by the barrel. She garnered chrysalises by the bucketful and watched how God brought life to his fairies of the great outdoors. Somewhere, somehow, she gained a prodigious amount of knowledge about these things. Without having completed a high school course, this little maid of mystery presented herself at the University of Oregon, where entrance requirements were waived because of her knowledge of geology, astronomy, and biology."

According to Mr. Bede and others who knew Opal as a girl, no one was ever heard to mention anything that would cause others to believe that she was an adopted daughter of the Whiteleys, and Mr. Bede says it was only with the publication of the diary by the *Atlantic Monthly* that relatives and friends received the first intimation that Opal claimed foster-parentage.

I asked Mr. Bede what Mr. Whiteley (Opal's real or foster father) thought about her claim to royal blood and he told me that the father thought "his daughter" had been caught in the meshes of some wily promoters.

Shortly after her diary was printed, Opal Whiteley left the United States very secretly, traveling with a confidential document—not an ordinary passport—signed by our Secretary of State and Sir Edward Grey of England of the British Foreign Office. Just how she was able to do this is amazing to Mr. Bede and others who knew the girl in her childhood; but obviously, if she was the bona fide daughter of American parents and not of Indian royal blood, we certainly have here evidence of the workings of the strange powers of the human mind, of which, I repeat, we know little.

At this writing, Opal Whiteley is reported to be living in England. But when Mr. Bede wrote his article a number of years ago he said: "When last definitely heard of, she had been accepted as a princess of India, through an alleged marriage of Henri d'Orléans, the 'angel' father of the diary." I asked him to explain how Opal had been accepted as a princess of India, if she was not in fact born one, and he said he couldn't. Then I asked him if he thought her constant thinking so, her very deep belief, had anything to do with it.

He replied: "Frankly, I do not know. It may be, for we haven't probed to the depths of the mind and don't know the extent of its powers."

Reading Mr. Sedgwick's own story of this strange girl, it would appear that he is also convinced that Opal's real parents were the Whiteleys and that her belief that she had been born of royal blood was pure fantasy. It may have been fantasy, but she was accepted by royalty, because Opal obviously knew a lot of secrets unknown to the average person. Here in his own words is Mr. Sedgwick's theory of how this nature child from Oregon made her vision come true.

I have a theory and hold to it. Among an infinitude of letters came one written by an American of French parentage, whose father, so he told me, was a sergeant in the Franco-Prussian War of 1870. Of this sergeant's regiment, the colonel or perhaps the general of his division was Prince Henri of Bourbon, and toward the close of his life the prince, traveling across America, stopped in Oregon to have a chat with his old soldier. Whether or not this is fact, I cannot say, but my correspondent had no doubt of it since, chief among his childhood memories, was the arrival of the prince at the cottage door of his father. "I sat on his knee," he told me, and I believed him.

Now, according to my theory, the visit of a prince of the blood to an Oregon hamlet was an event. The truth and the legend of it spread through the lumber camps and what is more likely than that such a tale captivated the mind of a lonely and imaginative child and that her daydreams centered about it. At the heart of every little girl, Cinderella sits enthroned, and with Opal, the legend grew to be true, and the truth magnified with the years, and finally permeated her entire mind, her fancy, and her life.

Such is my theory of Opal's childhood, but in after years the story becomes an attested record of fact and yet, to my thinking, loses nothing of its wonder thereby. Opal, who had come to know many notable people in New York and Washington, and who had been petted and patronized by them, grew sick of it all. She went to England, always making friends, took up the faith of her "father," and established herself in a Catholic community at Oxford. Then one day I had startling news of her. A friend of my youth, Mrs. Rosina Emmet Sherwood, mother of a playwright long since grown famous, wrote me asking whether it was possible to believe a correspondent of hers who stated that with her own eyes she had seen Opal sitting like the princess in the story in an open barouche driving in state down the streets of Allahabad, royal outriders clearing the way for H.R.H. Mlle. Francoise de Bourbon! The story was credible for it was true. I verified it beyond conjecture. First I wrote to Opal, who sent me a collection of photographs of her Indian tour. There she was perched in a howdah on an elephant's back, ready for a tiger hunt (Henri de Bourbon, be it noted, was famous for his bag of thirty-six tigers, and I laughed as I recalled Opal chanting French verses in honor of his victory), and there she stood the center of many another turbaned group. Photographs, as I have remarked frequently in the narrative, can be liars and many of them stem from Hollywood which hardly contradicts the term. I was not satisfied, and since Opal's narrative identified two of the greatest maharajas who had been her hosts, I wrote to both their courts. In due time two letters returned, emblazoned with regal crests, each informing me the writer's royal master bade the secretary reply that it had been his high privilege to entertain H.R.H. Mlle. Francoise de Bourbon, and that a series of fêtes had been given to do her honor. And the wonder of all this had not subsided when an unsolicited letter arrived from a lieutenant colonel of His Majesty's forces occupied at the moment with maneuvers at Aldershot, informing the editor with some asperity that the colonel himself had been honored by an order to attend Her Royal Highness at an official garden party given for her entertainment, and further he begged to ask who it was that had questioned the authenticity of the lady who had graced the occasion.

"I close this account on a melancholy note. In the journal which Opal sent to accompany her photographs, no vestige remained of the contagious fascination of an earlier day. She described things as they are. The dew of the morning had vanished. The hard sunlight of middle age beat down upon a world that everybody sees only too clearly. The fairy kingdom was now the playground of other children. Its gates were closed, and Opal stood without. But while she was still the Opal of the *Journal of an Understanding Heart,* she had had her vision, and the vision was true. There is no truth more certain than that which makes bright the heart of childhood."*

Some readers may question this weird story, but the facts are as related and obviously, as Mr. Sedgwick states, "The child who wrote Opal's diary believed in it. She knew it for her own."

No greater verification of the fact that there is genuine magic in believing can be offered than this strange story of Opal Whiteley, who believed she was born a princess of India and later was accepted as one.

*From *The Happy Profession* by Ellery Sedgwick. Copyright, 1946. Reprinted by courtesy of Little, Brown & Company and the Atlantic Monthly Press.

From early Biblical times to the present, there have been prophets, oracles, soothsayers, astrologers, and fortune-tellers. As a newspaper man (and I had the reputation of being a hard-boiled one), I have investigated a number of these so-called seers and while some were obviously charlatans of the first water, there were others who mystified me. Certainly there are many of these fortune-tellers who believe in their ability to foretell the future. Materialists will say that that is impossible. For myself, having spent years in research work, I am not so positive, for actually some of the great prophecies of the past have certainly been fulfilled.

Even though there are many who deride the ability of astrologers, fortune-tellers, and the like, there are millions of people in this world, including at the present day some of our greatest financiers, statesmen, and even, according to reports in recent years, members of our own cabinet, actors and actresses, and people in all walks of life, who believe in prophecies. No matter what my views are about the ability of anyone to foretell the future, I have long held the thought that it wasn't so much what the prophets foretold as it was the reliance of the subjects upon what the astrologer or soothsayer predicted for them that brought certain things to pass. In other words, a suggestion in the form of a prophecy was planted by the seer in the mind of the subconscious mind of the individual, which immediately went to work to make it come true. It was the power of suggestion working in the individual to make the prophecy a reality that finally produced the outcome. I believe that is what happened in the cases which I have cited.

I think of that great trouper, Marie Dressler, who probably evoked more laughter from a greater number of people than any other actress of modern times. Those who saw her in *Tillie's Nightmare, Tugboat Annie,* and various stage and screen appearances, will never forget that great personality; those of my readers familiar with her story know that Marie Dressler had a very hard time, suffering many privations before she became the great screen star known to millions. Whether true or not, I have read and heard that it was the advice and prediction of astrologers that landed Marie Dressler at the top.

In this connection, I relate the story of a strange experience

I had shortly before Miss Dressler's death. In explanation let me say that I firmly believe that when people get on a certain plane of thinking or are attuned with their subconscious minds, they automatically become *en rapport* with one another.

Shortly after I had written my little book, *T.N.T.—It Rocks the Earth,* it hit me in a flash that all great men and women had been using what I had outlined, and I set out to verify this by writing numerous outstanding men and women for their views and comments.

Marie Dressler, probably because I was her ardent admirer, was one of the first women selected. I heard her on the radio one night and knew instantly that she had a grip on "that something" which many people seek and seldom find, and I "knew" that if I wrote Miss Dressler, I would get a reply. My secretary, when I dictated the letter, volunteered the statement that Marie Dressler would never acknowledge receipt of it or my book. We even made a small wager, as I did later with several others. (It is common knowledge that very few great screen stars personally acknowledge letters from unknowns and it was upon this premise that those who wagered against me based their judgment.)

While I felt that Miss Dressler would immediately respond, I was astounded at her answer and comment, and especially at the sight of her enclosure, a check for twenty copies of my brochure. In her letter she said:

"Thank you so much. Oh! what a book, if used rightly. As I read through it and look back, which I very seldom do, and check up on my own life—it looks as though I had been going down the right path."

Naturally, now that this great woman has left us, her letter is among my cherished possessions, because I never had personal correspondence with a woman who had put so much of her great heart and soul into her work to cheer up humanity and yet who had had more personal trouble or who had put up a greater fight to reach the pinnacle of success.

Incidentally, there are two fine thoughts in her letter.

First, it is futile to dwell on or think about the past. It is apparent Miss Dressler discovered this a number of years before her death, realizing that she couldn't give full play to thoughts of future accomplishments if she cluttered up her mind with thoughts of the past.

Second, as she indicated in ordering extra copies of my brochure, she was always trying to help people, which may be a forlorn gesture in many instances; but she must have realized that the extending of such help did bring its own reward, even though it might have meant only personal satisfaction in knowing that a helping hand had been extended.

The name of Helen Keller is known to millions. This famous woman was a marvel to me. As the world knows, she was deprived of her sight, hearing, and speech when she was twenty months old, and yet she became an inspiration, through her talks and her many articles and books, to thousands who were less handicapped than she. The story of her life is fascinating, because when Helen Keller, through stupendous effort, learned to speak, she gave to the world a new vision of what handicapped people could do when once they believed in their ability to achieve. It is interesting to know that Helen Keller was a confirmed Swedenborgian. As many readers may know, Swedenborg lived in the early days of the eighteenth century and was perhaps one of the world's greatest mystics. He was a very unusual man, as he, too, could foresee the future, having anticipated the submarine, the machine gun, flying machines, and the horseless carriage that would go twenty miles an hour.

I don't know whether Swedenborg could be called a spiritualist, as we know the meaning of the word today, but he certainly had something far beyond the ken of the average person. He believed greatly in the power of the mind and had trances, visions, and strange dreams, which must have come from his subconscious mind.

Another outstanding woman of our time, who has been the subject of much controversy and whose name is known to millions because a motion picture depicting her life has been shown throughout the world, is Sister Elizabeth Kenny, who brought from Australia in 1940 an idea for treating polio victims. As a nurse in Australia, she discovered what is known as the "hot pack system," a method of applying hot-water packs to the afflicted portions of the polio victim's body. Despite the fact that she was ridiculed by many people professional and unprofessional, Sister Kenny, with her vision, persistently through what may even be said to be forceful methods, brought herself and her principles of treatment to the attention of the American public, and through her efforts established the Sister Kenny Institute at Minneapolis.

One has only to study the photograph of Sister Kenny's face to see in her rugged features the reflection of a powerful mind, which, once in action and aided by a ready tongue, would ultimately help her force her way to victory. In her native land she was fought at every turn, and it was only through the woman's sheer persistence that the medical profession of America finally gave her recognition. Few women of our day have been the subject of more controversy.

From what one reads and hears about Sister Kenny, she is convinced to the nth degree that her methods are right and practicable, and even though the whole world might attempt to discredit her, she could go marching bravely on. Here is an example of a woman with an idea, a singleness of purpose, and the utmost belief in the efficacy of her methods of treatment who has brought new hope for many polio sufferers throughout the world.

Now we come to a story which shows how the dynamic power in some women continues into their late years. The story concerns Captain Mary Converse, whose exploits were given in newspaper articles early in 1947. Mrs. Converse at seventy-five, a veteran of nearly 34,000 seafaring miles, wants to go to sea again. Born in Boston, she learned seafaring from her late husband, Harry E. Converse, owner of a steam yacht. As a junior navigator, she sailed the seven seas, obtained her second pilot's license in 1935, and her captain's license in 1940. Approximately 2,600 navy officers learned navigation from Mrs. Converse. She taught them in the dining room of her Denver home. Captain Mary Converse sails again!

While today a *Who's Who* of American women lists 10,222 biographical sketches selected from some 33,000 suggested names of outstanding women in business and the professions, including a number who are executives making more than $50,000 a year, our history recognizes no greater business woman than Lydia E. Pinkham. Her name may not be so well known to the women of today as to those of fifty years ago, but the business which she established and its product, Lydia

Pinkham's vegetable compound, still go merrily on. From a single idea, she built a huge business, which brought a return of millions and established a career the likes of which, for a woman, the world has perhaps never known.

Being a man, I know nothing about the efficacy of Mrs. Pinkham's vegetable compound, but I can remember as a boy often seeing a bottle of it in the family medicine chest. It was Mrs. Pinkham and her business associates who really modernized advertising, for she was one of the greatest of all advertisers. Ideas used in many advertisements today were originally voiced by Mrs. Pinkham. She tied in with much of her advertising a sort of homely philosophy embodying emotional appeals which seemed to have a way of penetrating to the hearts of her fellow-women and which resulted in not only millions of dollars in sales of her vegetable compound but also brought for more than half a century tons of enthusiastic testimonials to the laboratory at Lynn, Massachusetts.

Once more, in this extremely remarkable woman, is demonstrated what belief in personal achievement can and does accomplish. During Lydia Pinkham's early life, many people were interested in the manufacture of home remedies, and she, too, became interested in the idea. She started making her compound in her kitchen and for some time gave the mixture away to ailing women neighbors, only to awaken later to the fact that it could be sold. She then began promoting it. Like most people who start with an idea, she had many discouragements—lack of finances, the opposition of others, and manufacturing and sales difficulties. But nothing daunted this New England woman, for her tremendous driving force and enthusiasm reached and engulfed every member of her family. Especially was this true after her business really got going.

No book documenting the great power of believing would be complete without mention of Mrs. Mary Baker Eddy, also a New England woman, who built up that huge religious organization known as Christian Science. As almost everyone knows, Mrs. Eddy was faced with discouragement, strife, and the bitterest ridicule. But after she had caught the flash which gave to the world her *Science and Health with Key to the Scriptures*, she began to develop powerful leadership, a tremendous and unshaken belief in her teachings, and a dynamic personality which has left its imprint upon millions of people throughout the world. It has been said that few writings have done so much to influence the sciences of medicine and theology as hers. Christian Science is another practical demonstration of the power of believing.

The world will always be indebted to Florence Nightingale, who was greatly instrumental in saving the lives of thousands, and brought the nursing profession to the high standard now recognized by the entire world. Here again is an example of a woman who knew early in life what she wanted and who set out to realize her ambition. She had been born with a passion to nurse the wounded and the sick; at the time she undertook her great work, nursing was not even recognized as a profession.

She came from one of the richest families in England, but that meant nothing to this great woman. She started in by scrubbing the corridor floor at the Fliedner Nursing School in Germany and she soon showed that she could not only scrub floors but bind wounds, and with her encouraging talk, revive hopes. She, too, was fought at every turn, but being inspired with the vision of the destiny which she thought was hers, obstacles meant nothing to her. She hated bigots, believing that all should be cared for, irrespective of faith, color, or creed, and she had a quick tongue when aroused.

During the Crimean War, the males of the British War Office scoffed, saying that Florence Nightingale's work would only result in failure. Reluctantly they let the "madcap" have her own way. She organized, at her own expense, a private expedition of nurses and took them to Scutari, and even though the officers in charge of the hospital there wanted no woman to interfere with their work, interfere she did. Under the leadership of this originator of modern nursing, the women took over the handling of the hospital. Throughout her stay in the Crimea, her iron will constantly fought against a stone wall of opposition. Something had to give way, and this time it was the stone wall.

Some of the most powerful statesmen of Great Britain ridiculed this astonishing woman's work and did everything possible to stop her in her reforms; but her letters, "filled with dynamite," awakened her countrymen until she was adored everywhere. The story is told that when at the age of eighty-two, she became sick, her nurse tucked her into bed, only to have Florence Nightingale get out of her own bed and tuck in her nurse. At the age of ninety, just before she died, a friend asked her if she knew where she was and she replied, "I am watching at the altar of murdered men and I shall be fighting their cause."

When we think of martyrs, most people have in mind men who have died or been crucified or jailed for espousing causes in which they believed. Let us always remember there are many outstanding women of history who have suffered martyrdom as much as men, from Joan of Arc who was burned at the stake to women of modern times who fought and were jailed because of their efforts in furthering women's rights.

The name of Carrie Nation is probably becoming dim to the younger generation and perhaps is fading in the memory of many of the older generation. But during the years around the turn of the century, Carrie Nation was one of the greatest of women martyrs. Like many people imbued with an idea, Carrie Nation was convinced that she was "divinely" appointed to destroy the saloons and she set out to end the illegal sale of liquor in her own state of Kansas. Aided by some of her followers, Mrs. Nation succeeded by public prayer and denunciation in closing many illicit barrooms. When she saw this method was slow in its effectiveness, she took to wielding a hatchet, smashing bottles and beer kegs, and demolishing bar fixtures. She was constantly ridiculed and frequently jailed, but so thoroughly was she convinced of the righteousness of her cause that she accepted martyrdom gladly.

Surely everyone knows the story of Sarah Bernhardt. She had the temper of a tigress and yet history records her as one of the greatest emotional actresses of all times. She suffered innumerable failures in her early days on the stage, but she had a passion to make good, and make good she did; by the time she was twenty-four she was famous. She, a woman who smoked cigars and drank strong drinks, was a creature of extraordinary moods. She would visit cemeteries and sit on tombstones as if in grief for the departed. Sarah Bernhardt never appeared to be concerned with what people thought about her, and, as a matter of fact, she reveled in their comment. She was an individualist in the highest sense. The memory of her dramatic acting will probably go on forever.

Even though she had to have an artificial leg toward the end of her life, she continued her stage work, for nothing could change her lifelong belief that she was a supremely great actress—and she was to the end of her life in 1923.

Then there was that dynamic person, Madame Schumann-Heink, who was equally an exemplification of what belief can do, once the mind that carries it gets into action. She was inspired early in life, giving to the world her beautiful voice at the age of fifteen when she became an opera singer. She, too, became famous in the Old World, but when she came to America, it was the fulfillment of a dream that had burned fiercely within her for many years. Her heart was torn many times but even in the face of overwhelming odds, Madame Schumann-Heink always came smiling through.

Here was a woman whose oldest son had gone off in World War I to fight for the Kaiser while her other four boys were in the opposite trenches, but among those of us who heard her sing "The Star-Spangled Banner" in her quaint, foreign accent, there were many who took off their hats and wept. Over a national radio hookup, her voice became known to millions. She was beloved by everyone and she had that basic thing, born in most people but seldom aroused, the spirit of never quitting. It was at the age of seventy-two, when she was signed up as a successor to Marie Dressler, that the curtain rang down on this great performer.

No matter of what race, creed, or color, who has heard the wonderful contralto voice of Marian Anderson without being deeply moved and charmed by it! Yet few realize the very humble background of this great artist. I recall the story that as a child of six she wanted a violin; it was at the time she was learning that she could earn five or ten cents by scrubbing doorsteps in Philadelphia. If there ever was a woman who believed in her dreams, and who made them come true, it was Marian Anderson; she climbed to world fame and yet had to overcome, especially in our country, many handicaps and prejudices. Her triumph is one of the most dramatic in musical history. It was in Washington, D.C., on Easter Sunday of 1939, that this Negro girl of humble origin, standing before the Lincoln Memorial, thrilled an audience of 75,000 people, studded with cabinet members, senators, congressmen, and famous people in business and society. As we read the story of Marian Anderson, we must become convinced that she, too, succeeded through her belief, and that the great source of her inspiration came from her subconscious mind.

In this book are to be found numerous examples of men using the subconscious mind to achieve, but it is rather unusual to run across any written records of its use by women. Let me introduce here the story of a young woman who tells how her subconscious mind was directly responsible for her success. She is Angela Lansbury, the well-known young movie actress, who was interviewed by Mildred Mesirow for *Reach Magazine*. The interviewer tells us:

Angela Lansbury, the brilliant young screen star, aside from having beauty and dramatic ability, was also a girl with an exceptionally good brain. Angela's blond beauty has become familiar to millions of movie-goers through her masterly interpretation of the maid in *Gaslight,* her charming adolescent buoyancy in *National Velvet,* and her poignant interpretation of the tragic café singer in *The Picture of Dorian Gray*.

So varied a range of character-interpretation requires brains as well as beauty. Angela has both.

It was during a rest interval here [Hollywood] that she launched forth upon one of her favorite themes—her faith in her own destiny . . .

"Ah," she amended quickly, "I think perhaps I've phrased that badly. I don't mean anything magical or occult. Perhaps faith in the power of the subconscious mind would be a better way of saying it."

"In the manner of Tennyson, perhaps, or Stevenson?" was suggested.

"Exactly! Not that I think my abilities in any way resemble their genius, you understand. But I think I've learned how to tap the resources of the subconscious. Everyone knows that the subconscious mind stores all sorts of abilities, memories, and aptitudes we don't ordinarily utilize . . . What I'm trying to say is that, when you've learned how to draw on your subconscious powers, there's really no limit to what you can accomplish."

Angela has schooled herself in the technique of this

self-suggestion. Since first she chose acting as a career, she has constantly held in her mind a picture of what she aspires to achieve. She has even, she confessed, written down from time to time the goals she wants to reach. Obviously, she has tapped the reservoirs of creative material which few of us know how to use. Within the subconscious lie the materials of genius itself; of powers which, when properly recognized, may burst into the mental field of activity in patterns which surpass our conscious abilities . . .

"And how do you go about tapping your subconscious mind?" I asked.

"Heavens! I don't want to sound stuffy and highbrow, but it's really awfully simple. If you tell yourself over and over again that there's no limit to the creative power within you, that's about all there is to it. Honestly, I believe that's true. Whatever intelligence or creative force, or whatever it is, that resides in the world is like . . ." she waved a strong, beautiful hand expressively . . . "oh, like light or air, or something of that sort. It doesn't belong to *me*, especially. It's *there*, to be tapped and expressed by anyone who knows how to get at it.

"This isn't a cut-and-dried formula for success by any means," she continued. "It doesn't let you off hard work. You've got to keep plugging like mad, perfecting whatever kind of expression you've got; adding constantly to your skill, whether it's in acting or painting, or even making a dress. So that, when the chance for self-expression *does* come, when the time arrives for you to call on your subconscious power to express itself, you have a good set of tools for it to work with; a proper medium through which your creative urge can be portrayed. . . . Catch on?" she added with typical humor.

"About the suggestibility of the subconscious?" I prompted.

"Oh that! Well, when you're about to drop off to sleep, just tell yourself that tomorrow's the day you've got to surpass anything you did today. That, whatever demands are made upon you, all your abilities, all you've learned, perhaps things you've forgotten you ever knew—all these will be available to you. . . .

"Bearing in mind an actual mental picture of the situation is even better. If you're scheduled to do a screen test, for example, you *see* yourself acting-out that test better than anyone's ever done it before. Act it like mad in your mind! Be Duse; be Bernhardt! In your mental picture, be the best there is! And when the actual test comes off you find, often to your surprise, that you're acting better than you know how.

"The subconscious is a pretty dramatic factor in personality, I believe. It likes to act and sing and paint and express itself. It likes to surpass in anything it's called on to do. Your responsibility is to equip it with tools for expression, to give it a chance, and then make it an ally behind the scenes . . ."

Another example, and one of the most outstanding, is the story of how *Uncle Tom's Cabin* came into existence. It will be recalled that it was written by a wisp of a woman, Harriet Beecher Stowe, whose name will be remembered as long as there is American history. In 1850, Mrs. Stowe swore a solemn oath that she would write something "that would make the whole nation feel what an accursed thing slavery is." For two months she tried in vain to think of the story which was later to shake the world. In February, 1851, while she was attending communion service at the college church, there came to her mind the picture of Uncle Tom and of his death. According to the story, Mrs. Stowe went home in tears and when she had written out the scene of Uncle Tom's death and read it to her family, they, too, were in tears.

She did a great deal of research work in trying to secure factual material, but when she actually sat down to write, she needed none of it. The story obsessed her and literally wrote itself. Out of her subconscious mind surged long-forgotten memories and photographic impressions, which arranged themselves almost automatically in proper sequence on paper. Mrs. Stowe didn't think out these incidents and their background, she actually saw them; and while in her time little was known of the subconscious mind, it is obvious that it was the source of this story, which many claim brought on the War Between the States. Mrs. Stowe to her dying day insisted that it was God and not she who had written this book.

There are many famous women, including the Brontë sisters, Elizabeth Browning, Susan B. Anthony, Evangeline Booth, Jane Addams, who attained niches in the hall of fame. And today, while it is too early to tell the complete story, there are three women whose names will go down in history as having influenced and shaped the destinies of millions of Chinese. These are the famous Soong sisters, perhaps the best known of whom is Madame Chiang Kai-shek; the others married respectively Dr. H. H. Kung and Dr. Sun Yat-sen, both Chinese leaders.

As we come down to the present day and read the stories of women who have big ideas, we run across such people as Mrs. Matthew Astor Wilks, one of the richest women in the world and the daughter of the late Hetty Green, who, herself, amassed a fortune of over $67,000,000. Mrs. Wilks is following in the footsteps of her famous mother.

Then we have the account of Vera Nyman, which is literally another story of rags to riches. An idea, fifteen dollars, and a bathtub put her into a business for which Mrs. Nyman recently refused a million dollars. When she married her husband, Bernard, in 1920, she had the belief that she and her husband were going to make a million dollars. It took her twenty-seven years to achieve her objective of the million, but she had it within her grasp when a drug concern offered her that sum for her plant. Mrs. Nyman rang doorbells selling a liquid cleaner and later, by cooking chemical stews night after night in her own home, hit upon a combination of ingredients that would clean 90 per cent of painted surfaces. Her product today is known to millions of housewives and last year her sales topped $25,000,000. Mrs. Nyman, who day after day of making personal calls encountered more than 50,000 housewives, knows what it means to face discouragement, but her belief that she would ultimately make a million dollars never faltered.

Who's Who in America gives the stories of dozens of women who, as top-flight executives, writers, and professional women, receive from $25,000 to $100,000 a year. For example, here's the case of Mrs. George T. Gilmer of New Orleans, better known under the name of Dorothy Dix, the famous adviser to the lovelorn, who is reported to have received better than $75,000 a year. Then there is Mary A.

Bair, president of the Oliver H. Bair Company of Philadelphia, with a salary of $50,000. And by no means is Helena Rubenstein, who owns the famous cosmetic manufacturing company and whose income must be tremendous, to be overlooked.

Success stories could embrace dozens of women, such as Mary Dillon, president of the Brooklyn Borough Gas Company, who started in as a six-dollar-a-week office helper in the $5,000,000 corporation which she now heads; and Mrs. Ora H. Snyder of Chicago, who, about thirty-five years ago and with a capital of only five cents, began building up a candy business which centers around several shops and which was, at one time, worth more than a million dollars.

Add the story of Alice Foote MacDougall, president of the Emceedee Corporation Cortile, Inc., and many others like her who have built up huge businesses which have been managed as well as those headed by male executives.

An entire book could be written about women who have achieved fame and fortune in the field of radio and motion pictures as artists, writers, and executives. The name of Mary Pickford is known to millions, not only as a screen favorite but also as a motion picture corporation executive.

For a number of years Bertha Brainard was program director of the National Broadcasting System, with a salary that ran into five figures; she was said to be one of the highest paid women radio executives. It all came about through her getting an idea for feature radio programs. That was in 1922 and her first effort brought her a return of $50.

The whole world knows the story of Amelia Earhart, famous American aviatrix, who was lost with her plane in the South Pacific. While a teacher and a social worker, she became interested in aviation and became one of the world's greatest flyers. She was the first woman to cross the Atlantic in an airplane. In 1931 she made a solo flight across the Atlantic and four years later flew the Pacific alone from Honolulu to California.

One writer has said that the vast majority of American men do not believe that women are even their equals. But when we stop to examine the record, the list of women who have achieved success in every line of endeavor is an impressive one.

Here is the story of a great American woman who scored a double success—as a homemaker and a career woman. She is Mary Roberts Rinehart, who for more than forty years has thrilled the mystery-story fans of the world. Necessity forced her to make some money to retrieve the family fortunes which she and her doctor-husband had lost in a stock-market crash. With one hand, she wrote those great stories of fiction which gained her more than ten million readers, while with the other hand, she tended her babies and handled the details of housekeeping.

There are many women who have remained single simply because they feel deeply about marriage and are not willing to marry "just any man." But surely if this science of creative thinking can work for men, it can work also for women— even to the point of woman's actually creating an image of the man of her desires and literally bringing him into reality. In other words, if a single woman could visualize the kind of man she wanted and steadfastly held to the thought, in accordance with the principles of this science, she could bring the object of her mental picture into her presence. This may sound silly to some of my women readers, but it has been my good fortune to have given this science to many women who have used it most effectively. Therefore, if you are single and with your whole heart and soul you desire a certain type of man to walk into your life as a husband, merely picture him, not necessarily in physical form but in the abstract, setting forth in your thought projection the attributes that you would like to have in your man, and the day will surely come when you will meet him.

It seems to me that the women of today have the means of getting about everything they set their minds to. Certainly, opportunities are all around them. In fact, there never was a time in history when the world was so open to women as it is today. There are comparatively few fields among those which were formerly restricted to men in which women are not now represented. Today you'll find women in science, the fine arts, journalism, publicity, government, and various other branches, all working intelligently and with full knowledge of their duties and aware of their new opportunities and responsibilities.

There can hardly be any doubt that all of this is largely

because modern women are receiving the same education as men, with the result that they are not alone becoming acquainted with subjects hitherto regarded as essentially for men, but that their conscious or reasoning mind is being developed. In a way, it is perhaps superfluous for me to call women's attention to the importance and advantage of using their subconscious mind, for they have always used it. As a matter of fact, they are experts in the use of it—only they have always thought of it as woman's intuition. My point is that the subconscious is much more than intuition and that it possesses great forces which can be set in motion for the benefit not only of men but of women also, through the application of the power of dynamic believing. As I pointed out earlier, wonderful results are brought about by the conscious mind's conveying the will-to-do through believing to the subconscious, and this immediately sets the subconscious in action to carry out the desires of the individual.

Now the women of modern times have a unique advantage, I might say, a twofold mental advantage: to their subconscious mind the skilled use of which is characteristic of their sex and which has been highly developed and been their unconscious, though intuitive, guide through the ages, there has been added their conscious mind which has been specially developed by the scientific method of modern education. In my opinion, it is this combination which accounts for the speed with which women have acquired such rapid proficiency in so many of the so-called masculine subjects; and it is largely responsible not only for women's emerging from the traditional life within the home, but also for their entrance into the world where their view of people and practical affairs is broadened, made more objective and more understanding. Furthermore, it enables women in the home to have a better comprehension of the work of their men, as well as a deeper interest in the school studies and future life-work of their children.

My fundamental aim is to show how each person can develop his plus-powers, the seeds of which lie within his subconscious mind. It is these plus-powers which will enable you to obtain the things you want and the things you would like to be in addition to what you have and what you are already. By this new co-operation of the conscious and subconscious minds, you can gain those things which you feel deeply are necessary to your life and happiness, and also keep alive the feeling that no matter how long you live, you are undergoing personal development, are, in a word, progressing.

Always remember that the subconscious mind, in addition to being the seat of intuition, is a repository of great power and has inexhaustible resources. The more you call upon these resources, the more there are placed at your disposal. Remember also: the subconscious is ageless; it can never grow old or tired, and you can draw upon it all your life. The only thing you need is the power of believing—sincerely, strongly, and completely; once the subconscious has received your message and understands your desires and ambitions, it will be only a short time when your desire will be fulfilled and your ambition achieved. This book tells of the many men who have used this science and succeeded, but I would like to impress upon my women readers that they have the same two minds, conscious and subconscious, and that through them they can succeed just as men have. It is all a matter of believing and of co-operation of the two minds, according to the principles here set forth. The magic which comes from believing is real, for it has been demonstrated in the lives of some of the most successful. It can be demonstrated in your life—by your own personal believing.

CHAPTER IX

Belief Makes Things Happen

IN 1944 A POPULAR digest magazine had a story about a group of scientists in Chicago who were experimenting with moths. A female moth of rare species was placed in a room, and four miles away a male moth of the same species was released. In a few hours the male moth was found beating its wings against the window of the room in which the female was confined. The editor declared that he believed that ideas fly, with the sureness with which the female moth communicated her whereabouts to the male, across incredible barriers to the one mind for which they are originally intended.

Here is a simple experiment that will make you wonder whether the birds don't possess telepathic or clairvoyant power. In the off-season, put some scraps of bread in the backyard. There isn't a bird in sight. But hardly have you entered the house before birds begin to congregate. First come sparrows and wrens, then robins, and in two or three minutes the yard is filled with birds. Put out anything but food and not a bird appears. What brings them to your yard? How do they know the bread is food for them? Science can give no answers.

Edwin C. Hill in his broadcast of February 17, 1947, in talking about butterflies, made the statement that the more scientists investigate, the more they are becoming convinced that birds and insects have a wireless of their own or some other invisible manner of communication with one another. This has long been a theory expounded by nature students, and as a matter of fact, many books have been written on the subject, notably one by William J. Long, *How Animals Talk*.

It's interesting to note that during the last war, our Army Signal Corps, in experimenting with carrier pigeons and short-wave radio, found that the pigeons were affected by the radio waves and often, when confused, flew in circles and were lost.

When we consider that the swallows of San Juan Capistrano, California, fly away each October 23 and return each March 19 with unfailing punctuality; that tagged salmon released from Columbia River points spend four years in the Pacific Ocean, then consistently return to the spots from which they departed; that cats and dogs taken many miles from their homes have returned; that wild ducks and geese wing their way back to their original localities; that other inexplicable things are too numerous to mention here; are we not faced with the fact that there are wave radiations and telepathic forces also operating in the fish, bird, and animal kingdoms, in fact, in everything around us? Some writers claim that all living things have the means of communicating with each other, and in view of the Yale experiments, this may not be so farfetched after all.

Early in 1945 radio listeners heard the voices of blinded

soldiers telling of their experiences in "facial sight," through which they were able to detect objects in their paths through a sixth sense or kind of "mental radar." Dr. Jacob Levine, a Boston psychologist, who had charge of the school at Old Farms, in the Avon district of Connecticut, where war-blinded veterans were taught the use of this sixth sense, declared that he could not explain its mechanics, but he knew that it worked. This "facial sight" is based on the hypothesis that the body radiates definite rays of an unknown variety which, coming into contact with an object in front, assemble or group themselves in such form as to make a picture of it, after which they return, still bearing the picture, to the blinded person, who "sees" it through the sensation of the returning rays as they radiate through his body.

I have long had the conviction that various forms of telepathy or thought-transmission are used every day of our lives, far more than most people suspect. I believe that many great leaders, preachers, orators, executives, and so-called super-salesmen, some unconsciously and others thoroughly conscious of its workings, exercise the power to varying degrees. We meet a person, and before a word is spoken we experience a like or a dislike. What is it that causes the feeling to register but some form of thought-transmission? I have already stated that the only possible explanation of healing and affecting others at a distance is through the medium of this phenomenon, of which we are only now beginning to get a scientific explanation.

As I write, I have a mental picture of a famous lawyer in whose office I have often sat as he dictated letters concerning business affairs in which I was interested. When he dictated he always paced the floor, and his concentration was intense. Once I asked him why he stood while dictating and how it happened that his letters always accomplished the end intended. His reply was:

"In the first place, I think better on my feet. Then before I start dictating and during the whole period that I talk, I actually visualize before me the person to whom I write the letter. If I do not know him, I try to picture him as I think he may look. In both cases, I direct all my thought and words to him in person as though he were actually before me in the flesh and tell him mentally that my premises are right and should be followed by him."

A successful book saleswoman told me that if she was satisfied that a customer had the money and really wanted to purchase a book, but was hesitating between two choices, she would keep repeating to herself, but directing her thought to the customer, the title of the one best suited to that customer. She added that many of her sales were made by thought-directive power. An automobile executive told me that when he had a prospect who had the money to purchase, he always said to himself, "You're going to buy this car, you're going to buy this car"—and the prospect did.

I am aware that few people like to believe they are influenced by the silent thoughts of others when it comes to a matter of purchasing anything or doing something, but the fact remains that all of us are subject to this subtle influence, be it telepathy or anything else you want to call it. The fact remains, too, that this invisible power exists, and a little experimenting on your part will convince you that it is both formidable and active.

I am certain that mothers use it on their children and often children use it on their parents. Not infrequently husbands and wives use it on one another without the knowledge of either one. This is especially true where a man and wife are closely attuned to one another. You who are married and have never used this science, have a new field to explore.

One of the most striking examples of this subtle influence in action came to my attention several years ago. The president of a company that I had been helping was dissatisfied with his sales manager, but because of many years of service did not wish to discharge him. "I was at my wits' end," he told me, "when I suddenly got the idea that I could suggest to him mentally that he ought to resign his job and become a salesman instead of remaining as manager. I thought about it for hours one night, but I nearly fell off my chair when the first thing next morning he came into my office, saying that he would like to resign as manager as he felt that he could make more money by getting out on the street as a salesman. I don't know whether I was guilty of using some sort of magic, but my conscience is clear, because the man today is making twice as much money as he did when sales manager and he's much happier, and we're all going to town."

In this connection, here is another story, that of a man and wife who came to see me. The man told me that until a few months before our meeting he had been one of the largest clothing manufacturers in the Middle West, but had sold out and was now traveling the country. His story, taken from a memorandum transcribed at the time, is briefly as follows:

"For more than thirty years I had been a member of one of the largest and oldest secret organizations in the world which embraces this theme of believing from A to Izzard, but I, like thousands of others, never had my mind opened to it and I never realized the 'truths' contained therein. However, several years ago I attended a series of lectures on the subject of mind control and my eyes were opened for the first time to what a wonderful power man could make available for himself if he saw fit to do so. I could see how it would work in our business to tremendous advantage and I used it. Needless to say, our business started to increase as soon as I put it to work and it has been increasing ever since. During the depression when firms like ours were having a terrific struggle we consistently made money, and when I sold out my interests I guess I can say, with all modesty, that I was at the top."

At this point his wife entered the conversation, saying: "My husband wouldn't openly scoff at me when I talked this subject and what I had learned at the lectures before he started, but he gave me to understand that he believed I was wasting my time. I just knew there was something to it and I was certain that if my husband could get hold of it—it would mean a great deal more business for him. I talked to him about attending the lectures until I was tired and then one day I realized I was doing the wrong thing. Instead of talking to him I should use the very science which I had been taught. I went at it with a vengeance. Both my daughter and I several times a day kept repeating to ourselves mentally, 'Dad is going to go, Dad is going to go.' It took us nearly three weeks, but Dad did go."

Here the husband broke in, saying: "You speak about your tap-tap idea. Well, she certainly worked it on me. When she first talked about what she had heard at the lectures, I just couldn't believe them to be true. I had been brought up in a very practical business world and I couldn't get myself to believe in many of the so-called abstract things. However, one day 'something' impelled me to make up my mind to go with her. I didn't know at the time that the 'something' was my wife's mental suggestion and I had no idea that she and my daughter had been 'working on me.' However, it was the greatest thing that ever happened to me. After the first lecture I did some experimenting and our business began to improve and continued to improve until the day I sold out.

"Don't get me wrong. I am not religious in an orthodox sense, and what I talk about is not goody-goody stuff, but an exact science. What we think or contemplate develops into reality. We radiate our thoughts, perhaps unconsciously, to others, and we affect them. We give forth vibrations of dislike or hatred which we engender in ourselves—and, bingo, they come right back and floor us. All one needs to do is to study and understand the law of cause and effect, and it all becomes plain. Thought has been referred to as a powerful unseen influence, and so it is. There are so few people you can talk with on this subject. Most people ignorant of the subject look at you askance when you mention something about it, and now I understand why the Master spoke in parables. However, I've reached the conclusion that it will not be many years before people generally are into the subject up to their ears, for there are thousands of enlightened people who are recognizing that we are on the threshold of great developments dealing with thought power, and the number is rapidly increasing. I wonder why more men in the business world don't catch hold of it and apply it in their businesses, but I guess that most of them are like I used to be—they keep their minds closed and no one ever takes the trouble to work on them as my wife did on me. All a person has to do is to believe, earnestly and sincerely, that such a power of mind exists and then conscientiously apply the science. It's all just as you say: when one starts tapping the subconscious mind, your own or others, the bricks fall into place as though by magic. Does it work? And how!"

Alfred F. Parker, a highly respected general insurance agent in the Pacific Northwest, has given me permission to quote a letter he wrote to me in 1937, in connection with the use of this science. I do not know whether Mr. Parker is even interested in the subject of telepathy, but I do know that he thoroughly believes in the efficacy of belief. His letter speaks for itself:

Recently I had opportunity to put into further practice your tap-tap idea, and I thought that you might be interested in knowing the circumstances. I have a small son who is quite naturally the apple of my eye. On December 29, 1936, he picked up some obscure infection and for days he lay desperately ill in the hospital. There was grave doubt that he would live. I was in terrible anguish, but I resolved to meet the situation as best I could. Taking a tip from you, I put his picture on my desk and carried another in my pocket. Every hour of the day I kept looking at them and repeating to myself, "He will recover. He will recover." At first I felt I was lying to myself, as he hardly seemed to have an even chance. However, I kept it up and gradually found myself believing what I kept repeating. At just about that time, thanks to the best medical and nursing attention and some of a friend's blood transfused into him, the boy actually *did* begin to recover. He is now at home and regaining his strength fast. It may have been a mere coincidence that the time when empty words began to turn into belief was the time when recovery began, but at least such coincidence is worthy of note.   —

Some people have had the experience of walking into a darkened room and feeling the presence of someone there, even before a word was uttered. Certainly, it couldn't have been anything else but the vibrations of some unseen individual that indicated his presence to the other person. Evidence of telepathy? What do *you* think? It is maintained that if the first person in the room will, at the entry of the second person, think of something entirely foreign to himself and dismiss from his mind all thought of the possibility of his discovery, the second person will not sense his presence. There are thousands of people who have thought of someone, only to hear from them or see them shortly thereafter, and they have given no heed to the phenomena involved. These experiences are usually considered coincidences; but when we properly consider the power of thought, do we not have the real explanation? I cannot help but feel that anyone with an open mind and willing to read and experiment for himself, will sooner or later come to the conclusion that the phenomena of psychokinesis and telepathy are realities, and, as investigators have pointed out, that these powers are latent in everyone, though developed to varying degrees.

Hudson, in his *Law of Psychic Phenomena*, originally published in 1893, recounted numerous experiments to prove the existence of telepathy, among them being the use of playing cards. One member of a group of people was blindfolded, after which a card was selected by another member upon which the others present were told to concentrate. The blindfolded person was then asked to name it, according to the first mental impression he received. The results were further proof of the validity of telepathy.

Here is a simple experiment that may be carried on by only three people. Cut five colored slips of paper from a magazine, each about half an inch wide and three inches long. The more vivid the colors, such as bright red or electric blue, the better, but be sure to have them quite distinct from one another. One person should then place them fan-wise between the thumb and forefinger of his right hand, as you would hold a hand of cards. Let either of the other two people touch any one of the colored slips without being seen by the third person. Immediately after this the first person who holds the slips concentrates his mind on the colored slip selected, with a view of communicating the information to the mind of the third person who is then requested to indicate which slip was touched by the second person. It should be made clear to the third person that his decision must be immediate and spontaneous, and that his mind should either be blank or thinking of something entirely remote from the experiment. That is, he should not attempt to guess, deliberate, or try consciously to think of the color of the slip selected, but should act immediately upon the first mental impulse he receives. The number of times the third person will name the colored slip selected by the second person will astound you. With a little practice, people—who are more or less *en rapport*, such as husband and wife, the husband holding the slips and the wife acting as the third person after some second person has previously indicated a choice—will make an even higher score of success. I have seen this done twenty to thirty times without a single miss. Here again belief must come into play. The holder of the slips must possess not alone the ability to maintain an unwavering concentration, but the strong belief that he can transmit the image of the color to the mind of the third person.

Let me interpose a word of caution. This experiment, as well as others outlined in this book, should never be attempted in the presence of scoffers or those who profess a disbelief in psychic phenomena, for, with their negative thoughts, they may confuse and obstruct the free flow of your own, especially if their skepticism is aggressive. Always remember that belief is a power operating destructively or constructively, depending upon the end to which it is employed. Recall Dr. Rhine's discovery of how disbelieving could depress the results in the psychokinesis tests. In addition, note this: Dr. G. R. Schmeidler of the Harvard Psychological Clinic, where extensive experiments in telepathy have been made, has pointed out that subjects who maintain that telepathy is a myth or that the hypothesis is false, invariably show scores far below those of chance. Once more we see in action the magic of believing. Believe that it will work, and it will. On the contrary, believe that it will not work, and it will not!

The great French astronomer and scientist, Camille Flammarion, an early exponent of thought-transmission, held somewhat to the theory later advanced by Professors Eddington and Jeans. He claimed that there was mind not only in human and animal life, but in everything—in plants, minerals, even space—and he declared that mind gleams through every atom.

Early in 1947, Dr. Phillips Thomas, previously referred to, publicly announced that upon retiring he intended to devote his time to research in the field of telepathy. Dr. Thomas said:

"You may think I'm crazy, but I intend to devote my time to research in this field when I retire in two years. We can't conceive scientifically how this [telepathy] could come about, but neither can we explain the apparent success of 'mind readers.' "

This announcement caused the Portland *Oregonian* to comment editorially:

The other day in this newspaper there appeared an interview with a successful professional man who spoke of his impending retirement, and added that he should thereafter devote his time to research in the strange field of telepathy and kindred phenomena, generally aggregated as extrasensory perception. Before you exclaim, "Ha, another crackpot!" pray reflect that Dr. Phillips Thomas is an eminent scientist who for many years has been research engineer with the Westinghouse Company. Now he elects to become an explorer of that last dark continent, the human mind, in which, beyond peradventure, more marvels and mysteries are hidden than ever were discovered in Africa.

It must be evident to the veriest skeptic that Dr. Thomas, international authority on electronics, is convinced—by evidence not lightly to be dismissed—that in our sedulous application to what may be called conventional science we have rather stupidly neglected those challenging phenomena which in times past bore the stigma of sorcery and witchcraft . . .

The proper and rational attitude toward the seeming phenomena of the mind—if that is what they are—is one of scientific inquiry which, though rigorously exacting, will not resist conviction when incontestable proof has been obtained. Actually there can be no such thing as a supernatural phenomenon, but only the manifestation of natural law as yet unknown to us. Nor is it without precedent, this decision of a distinguished scientist to attempt penetration of the unknown continent of the mind . . . Dogmatic disbelief, not infrequently manifested by scientists toward telepathy and similar manifestations, is far from being a scientific attitude.

What profit to mankind is there in the quest to which Dr. Thomas presently shall address himself? This is a question most difficult of reply, for it may be that the inner secrets are, indeed, inviolable. But if of this research comes a better understanding of ourselves, and of the forces which are latent in mind, it might be that the knowledge would liberate more of happiness for the race.

In the last couple of years much has been written about Robert R. Young, the aggressive and energetic chairman of the board of the Chesapeake & Ohio Railway, and his plans for railroad improvement and development. While I have never seen anything in print stating that Mr. Young utilizes the subconscious, I think that anyone knowing anything about the subject would conclude from these articles about him that Mr. Young relies greatly upon it for his ideas. In an article appearing in *Life* magazine early in 1947, it was stated that Mr. Young believed in "extrasensory perception" and that he could "become almost mystical about getting off by himself and 'feeling a truth.' "

Whether it be mind, as we understand the general usage of the word, or whether it be electrical vibrations of some kind, it is the phenomena themselves with which we deal, call them what you wish. The conclusion is that they embrace and pervade everything.

So when we consider the subconscious mind of a single individual as being only an infinitesimal part of the whole and the vibrations therefrom extending to and embracing everything, we get a better understanding of the workings of psychokinesis, telepathy, and kindred phenomena.

In explaining psychokinesis, Dr. Rhine points out that there must be a mental attitude of expectancy, concentration of thought, and enthusiasm for the desired results if a person is to be successful in the experiments. Again we have the magic of believing at work. The subject must have a prior belief that he can influence the fall of the dice.

That belief is the basic factor in the ability to demonstrate psychokinesis (control of mind over matter) and telepathy was more recently confirmed in experiments at Duke University as reported in the *New York Herald Tribune* by its science editor, John J. O'Neill. Mr. O'Neill declared that these experiments proved that it was possible to "kid" a person out of his power to demonstrate psychokinesis and telepathy.

He told of how a young woman, by distracting the attention of one of the young men attempting to control the fall of the dice, and by scoffing at his professed ability to demonstrate his power of mind to direct matter, succeeded in injecting such a strong negative factor that she weakened his belief in himself and ruined his score for the day. Mr. O'Neill made an interesting speculation about this when he went on to say: "The converse of this experiment, still to be made, in which a test would be made of the possibilities for improving the score by a confidence-inspiring 'pep' talk offers interesting possibilities."

At this writing, the outcome of such an experiment is not known, but in view of the thousands of experiments previously made at Duke and other universities, it is apparent that scores improve when the experimenters *believe* and are confident of the results. Also, nothing is more logical than that "pep" talks should be helpful to those who lack confidence or belief, and thus they should improve their scores.

If golf shots can be influenced by mental attitudes or proper visualization, and the "galloping ivories" turn up at the mental command of the players, who is there now to gainsay that events are not influenced by thought and that before us is a field that is gradually yielding to modern man some of the secrets of the ancient mysteries? Do not the experiments at Duke University prove that the so-called luck factor is in reality an influence brought about by powerful thought vibrations, rather than coincidence or chance? Writers, long before the experiments at Duke, declared that the luck factor came about from a determined mind—a combination of visualizing, concentrated thought, willing, and believing. Think about this in connection with yourself and the goals you have set for yourself, for in it is the primary secret of this science.

Anyone who has associated with the garden variety of parlor gambler knows that the word "hot" is often applied to card players or "crap shooters" when they have a winning streak. When the "hot" period wears off, the gamblers either quit the games or begin to lose. What is this "hot" period? Nothing more than an all-knowing feeling, a deep-rooted belief that they can win. Even in gambling the magic of believing plays a major role.

Of course, this book is not written for professional gamblers but for sincere men and women who wish to succeed in life. The material referring to the games of chance is included only to provide further evidence that with concentrated thought, expectancy, and steadfast belief, we actually set in motion vibratory forces that bring about material manifestations.

As stated previously, charms, amulets, discs, talismans, etc., have no power in themselves, but those who firmly believe in them unquestionably tend to develop the kind of force or power now known as psychokinetic. I have tried to make plain how this power through belief can be developed and to take you up the ladder as far as you wish to go. It is necessary, though, to point out that it is easy to lose one's belief or faith. Thousands have risen to great heights of success, only to stumble, roll, or fall to undreamed-of depths. Others, seeking health, have appeared to be more or less miraculously cured, only to find that in later years or even months there is a recurrence of their ailments. There are many weakening factors and influences—all suggestive in nature—which we, in unguarded moments, allow to slip into our subconscious minds, and which, once there, begin their destructive work and undo all the good accomplished by our constructive forces. So step out in front, head toward the sun. Keep facing it and the dark shadows will not cross your path.

The writer knows that it is difficult for the average person who knows nothing of this subject to accept the idea that all is within; but surely the most materialistic person must realize that as far as he himself is concerned, nothing exists on the outside plane unless he has knowledge of it or unless it becomes fixed in his consciousness. It is the image created in his mind that gives reality to the world outside of him.

Happiness, sought by many and found by few, therefore is a matter entirely within ourselves; our environment and the everyday happenings of life have absolutely no effect on our happiness except as we permit mental images of the outside to enter our consciousness. Happiness is wholly independent of position, wealth, or material possessions. It is a state of mind which we ourselves have the power to control—and that control lies with our thinking.

"Consider that everything is opinion, and opinion is in thy power," said the great philosopher, Marcus Aurelius Antoninus. "Take away then, when thou choosest, thy opinion, and like a mariner, who has doubled the promontory, thou wilt find calm, everything stable, and a waveless bay."

A modern version of this is found in the statement of the seventy-eight-year-old man previously quoted, who said:

"Distress ensues only when developed by conscious mental attitudes. Disappointments, suppressions, melancholy, depressions, etc.—all are emotional excitations or suggestions from a mode of thinking those things. If these emotional tendencies are resisted and will-power is asserted to prevent such influences reaching our consciousness, the foundation of the thought disappears and consequently the distress vanishes. It will be noted that this weakness to resist repressing thoughts and imaginations arising from emotional reflex develops from failure of self-control and command of the situation as thought presents it. Stop thinking! Refuse to think that idea or way. Assert yourself to be the creator and boss of your own habits of thought—in fact, become unconquerable. No one ever defeated a resolute will. Even death stands still before such a will."

Emerson said: "What is the hardest task in the world? To think." Obviously this is so, when one considers that most of us are victims of mass thinking and feed upon suggestions from others. We all know that the law of cause and effect is inviolable, yet how many of us ever pause to consider its workings? The entire course of a man's life has many times been changed by a single thought which, coming to him in a flash, became a mighty power that altered the whole current of human events. History is replete with the stories of strong-minded, resolutely willed individuals, who, steadfastly holding to their inner convictions, have been able to inspire their fellow-man, and in the face of tremendous and determined opposition have literally created out of nothing great businesses, huge empires, and new worlds. They had no monopoly of thought-power. You and every man and woman have it. All you have to do is to use it. You will then become the person you envisage in your imagination, for with the working of the law of cause and effect, you bring into your life the new elements which your most dominant thoughts create within and attract from without.

Positive creative thought leads to action and ultimate realization, but the real power, much more than action itself, is the thought. Remember always: "Whatever man can conceive mentally, he can bring into materialization." Health, wealth, and happiness must follow if the proper mental pictures are created and constantly maintained, for the law of cause and effect is immutable.

"Know Thyself." Know your power. *Read* and *reread* this book until it becomes a part of your daily life. Faithfully use the cards and the mirror technique and you will get results far beyond your fondest expectations. Just believe that there ‘is genuine creative magic in believing—and magic there will be, for belief will supply the power which will enable you to succeed in everything you undertake. Back your belief with a resolute will and you become unconquerable—a master of men among men—*yourself*.